Inclusion Confusion

Inclusion Confusion

A *Guide to Educating Students With Exceptional Needs*

Fern Aefsky

CORWIN PRESS, INC.
A Sage Publications Company
Thousand Oaks, California

For information address:

Corwin Press, Inc.
A Sage Publications Company
2455 Teller Road
Thousand Oaks, California 91320

SAGE Publications Ltd.
6 Bonhill Street
London EC2A 4PU
United Kingdom

SAGE Publications India Pvt. Ltd.
M-32 Market
Greater Kailash I
New Delhi 110 048 India

Printed in the United States of America

Library of Congress Cataloging-in-Publication Data

Aefsky, Fern.
    Inclusion confusion : a guide to educating students with exceptional needs / Fern Aefsky.
        p.   cm.
    Includes bibliographical references
    ISBN 0-8039-6283-5 — ISBN 0-8039-6284-3 (pbk.)
    1. Mainstreaming in education—United States. 2. Handicapped children—Education—United States. 3. Special Education—Law and legislation—United States.   I. Title.
    LC4031.A54   1995
    371.9′046′0973dc20   95-16609

This book is printed on acid-free paper.

95 96 97 98 99 10 9 8 7 6 5 4 3 2 1

Corwin Press Production Editor: S. Marlene Head

Contents

Preface

This book is intended to provide practitioners with a clear understanding of what inclusive education is and what it means to teachers, parents, students, administrators, and boards of education. It is also intended to clarify the inclusion confusion that currently exists in educational realms. The focus is on baseline information for dealing with the delicate balance of teaching disabled and nondisabled children as an integral part of educational reform movements.

The rules and regulations for educating all children in an appropriate setting as well as current legal cases on inclusion issues are the bases for discussions of educational restructuring. A step-by-step outline for planning inclusion programs is included, as are strategies for teachers and administrators to implement and support sound educational practices for structuring an enhanced learning environment for all children.

The issue of inclusion is a concern for a variety of consumers in the educational world. Incorporating children with a variety of disabilities into the regular classroom can frighten and confuse teachers, parents, and administrators. Guidelines, legalities, strategies, and techniques for developing and implementing inclusion programs for children for the correct reasons are the focus of this book.

This book differs from others on inclusion because it incorporates educational reform initiatives of restructuring and teaching all children in a productive manner by maximizing the resources of teachers, children, and schools. The philosophical base is derived from practitioners in school districts throughout the country and is tied into research, but mainly it assists practitioners in learning strategies and techniques found successful by other practitioners.

The general goal of this book is to provide information that helps people to stop labeling children, curricular reforms, and programs, and to start merging the knowledge of educators to teach children in an appropriate manner for the 21st century. Society is not separate from schools, and schools need to recognize societal needs and adjust instruction to meet the needs of children in a less-than-perfect society. Focusing on maximizing the school day to encourage children to learn, and eradicating ancient practices based on tradition rather than good practice, is one way of helping all children to learn in a diverse society.

The commonality of language among educators will allow school staff to begin building communication bridges with parents of students. Energy must be focused on working with the students as they come to school, having great expectations, and working with parents when possible to provide youth support for instructional progress.

Practitioners at every school level will be interested in this book, including superintendents, members of boards of education, administrators, teachers, and support staff. This book will provide college students with a practical document to supplement research materials in training for teaching a diverse student body. Lesson planning would be enhanced by incorporating the strategies discussed, from kindergarten through 12th grade.

This book is readable and understandable, and it easily can be used to plan, evaluate, and change educational practices for disabled and nondisabled children. Parents can use the book to support their roles as advocates for their children based on accurate information.

The significance of this book is its focus on bridging educational reform components in restructuring schools to teach all children. Instead of confusing practitioners who do not have time to integrate philosophies and terms whenever a "new" philosophy becomes the "ticket" to success, practical information from teachers and administrators is integrated to support school staffs in teaching their assigned students with the best options possible. This book does not claim to provide all the answers, but it does suggest strategies, techniques, and possibilities for administrators and teachers to change how they meet the needs of all students.

The book helps to create an understanding of what inclusion means because people continually define it differently. In the first chapter, information is given about the recent history of laws supporting the rights of disabled children to a free, appropriate education and the mass confusion of how to meet the needs of all children, disabled and nondisabled, in schools. Clarification of mandates, concerns, and goals are discussed.

Chapter 2 reviews legal cases regarding the inclusion movement. Discussions of important cases and the implications for schools and students are detailed.

Chapter 3 provides information on how to plan inclusive practices in any school based on case-specific and systemic needs of the school district. Information disseminated is from teachers and administrators involved in pilot programs in the Monticello Central School District, New York. Problems, concerns, successes, and needs for planning, implementing, and evaluating programs are discussed.

Chapter 4 targets teacher strategies on a kindergarten through 12th-grade level, which will assist teachers in developing program components. Sample lessons, incorporating educational initiatives, provide the reader with ways of implementing components for shared students.

Chapter 5 discusses ways to enhance education by communicating ideas and practices between and among teachers, administrators, and parents. The development of a parent university program is a focal point of increasing parental involvement in schools.

I would like to thank the administrators in the Monticello Central School District, without whom the pilot programs could not have been actualized, and all the teachers, speech therapists, and support personnel involved in the inclusion pilot and task force. Special thanks to Eileen Casey, Superintendent, Stan Hersh, Director of Pupil Personnel Services, and Harold Diamond, Principal.

And extra special thanks to my dad, Harold Heller, who taught me to follow dreams!

FERN AEFSKY, ED.D.
Monticello, New York

About the Author

Fern Aefsky has worked as a special education teacher for 7 years and as an administrator of early childhood and special education programs for 10 years. She created an inclusive preschool and kindergarten program in Virginia in 1986, before the word *inclusion* was used by professionals. She has always worked as an advocate for children, both with disabilities and without specified needs, because she believes all children need a nurturing environment in which to gain skills. She received her Ed.D. degree in educational administration from Nova Southeastern University in 1995, and her dissertation was an applied research project on inclusion. Gathering information for her doctoral studies allowed her the opportunity to obtain firsthand information on inclusion from parents, teachers, and administrators and to see how programs for children could work for student success.

1

Clarifying Issues of Inclusion

The topic of inclusion is one that is receiving much attention in educational settings. Inclusive education has arrived on the doorstep of every school. The belief that inclusion means that all children must be educated in the regular classroom is a myth that is dividing educators and putting them into adversarial roles.

A significant problem with the inclusion movement is the assumption that educators agree on a definition of inclusion as a way of educating children. Inclusion was publicized as a new mandate in the late 1980s and early 1990s, frightening professionals and parents. Thoughts of children being placed in classrooms without concern for individual students' needs was a prospect that concerned all members of the educational community.

A Brief History of Inclusion

In the mid- to late 1980s, inclusion began gaining educators' attention based on information shared from Canada. In Canada, there was no federal law equivalent to Public Law 94-142, the Education for All Handicapped Children Act of 1975, renamed the Individuals with Disabilities Education Act (IDEA) in 1990. The closest legal policy is

1

found in the Canadian Charter of Rights and Freedoms (1982), which states that each citizen has the right to "equal protection and equal benefit . . . without discrimination based on race, national or ethnic origin, color, religion, sex, age, or mental or physical disability." Provinces developed laws within this context pertaining to the education of students with disabilities.

In 1982, Montreal developed a program that included all disabled children in regular class settings. The program's reputation grew and began a Canadian response to inclusive practices (Crawford & Porter, 1992).

In 1986, the Province of New Brunswick passed Bill 85, which specifies that pupils with disabilities shall be placed with nondisabled peers in regular classroom settings "to the extent that is considered practicable by the board having due regard for the education needs of all pupils." This began the Canadian focus on full inclusion, where alternatives to the regular classroom are looked at for a disabled student only after a serious attempt is made to make inclusive education a success. If an alternative setting is recommended, it is for a specified amount of time, and a plan to return the student to the regular classroom is implemented from the onset of the alternative program.

The state of Vermont became a leader in attempting to bring about inclusion as part of an educational reform initiative in this country. Legislation (Act 230) has merged resources formerly designated to regular and special education to serve all students in the general classroom setting. The inclusion initiative states high expectations for all students, does not distinguish between "regular" and "special" education, encourages the creation of planning teams, and supports administration in facilitating planning teams by allowing time for shared planning and staff development.

An inclusive project was initiated by Syracuse University in 1990, driving a statewide systems change project. This project involved including severely disabled children in the regular classroom. Training sessions and information were shared from this project, and some districts developed programs as a result of it; however, the first state-supported inclusion conference was held in May 1993. This conference provided a forum for presenters from the Syracuse project, districts with inclusive programs, and state agencies, and for discussion of legal support and questions of inclusive practice. At this conference, some school district presenters shared innovative inclusive practices that were considered typical educational service provision by other districts. There was a significant variance in what school personnel considered inclusive practices presented at this conference.

Between 1989 and 1992, the federal government audited many states' programs for disabled students, among them Maryland, Florida, and New York. In 143 of 165 districts monitored, districts failed to place disabled students in the least restrictive environment with nondisabled peers, as required by the Individuals with Disabilities Act (*Special Education Report*, 1993). State departments of education were told to look at these practices and create policies that were consistent with federal regulations.

As the inclusion movement grew, districts in other states began developing inclusive board policies. In Glens Falls, New York, the inclusion policy contained a vision statement that the total education of all students is a shared responsibility of the school, family, and community. A commitment of the district was to provide students, staff, parents, and the community with the necessary, ongoing support through education, time, resources, and recognition.

In June 1992, a report was made to the board of education in Bainbridge-Guilford district (New York) by the inclusion committee. This committee met for 1 year and submitted a 5-year plan for inclusive practices to be implemented. It contained staff needs, training suggestions for teachers, and evaluation components.

In Howard County (Maryland), a report to the board of education outlined long-range plans for inclusion (Office of Special Education, 1993). Staff development, resources of time and money, administrative support, and collaboration were identified components of the proposal.

The New York State School Boards Association has been working with the state regents board in trying to understand teacher, parent, administrator, and student concerns while investigating how state districts (1,500 of them) are dealing with inclusion. Statements such as these imply that inclusion is a separate program or mandate, rather than a reconsideration of regulation implementation.

In Palm Beach County (Florida), an inclusive philosophy statement adapted from Florida's Strategic Plan (1993) was adopted by the board of education in December 1994 that states that "successful inclusion benefits all when there is adequate training and support, and a commitment to provide each student with an appropriate education."

However, in these and other states, the implementation of inclusive programs was perceived to be poorly planned and executed in schools, leaving teachers, administrators, and parents confused and concerned about educating disabled and nondisabled students.

The Americans with Disabilities Act (ADA) (1991) and IDEA created an awareness of the educational rights of disabled children. Although inclusion was described as a new mandate by educators, lawyers, and the media, P.L. 94-142, the Education for All Handicapped Children Act of 1975, mandated that all children were entitled to a "free, public education, . . . in the least restrictive environment [LRE]." Once a child was determined to be eligible for services as a disabled child, the law required that services and the location of those services be based on individual needs. A regular classroom setting, with support, was the first consideration for providing services because the classroom is the least restrictive environment. If this option cannot adequately meet the child's educational needs, only then can a more restrictive setting be considered in delivering special education services to a student.

These regulations were being interpreted by school districts as mandating that all children, regardless of disability, be educated in the regular classrooms in their neighborhood schools. Unfortunately, some school districts in many states have decided to assign all students, regardless of disabling condition, to regular classes, guided by boards of education, superintendents, parent groups, and other perceived political influences. These districts have gone "cold turkey" and stated that a change in the delivery of special education services must occur overnight. In many situations thus described, the central administration of the school district believed that this changeover would comply with perceived new regulations and prevent legal challenges, thus saving money for the district. In reality, this instantaneous change has created resentment, anger, and confusion for all participants. This philosophical change has resulted in a chaotic educational environment for the students that the systemic change was supposed to help.

The Debate Over Inclusion

Inclusion differs from mainstreaming in that mainstreaming is an educational term that provides disabled students the opportunity to be placed in a regular class based on the student's ability to keep up with work assigned, with some modifications. Instructional support and related services are typically provided outside of the regular education setting. Integration, a term popularized in the 1980s, was used to indicate the placement of a disabled child in a special class, in a typical school, where the student could participate in some activities with nondisabled peers (e.g., art, music, library, assembly programs). Special education services were usually provided in a special education class. Teachers recommended that disabled students have a consistent classroom environment with little transition. This fragmented approach caused children to become lost in the system (Dawson, 1987). A dual system was then created in which disabled children became a separate entity in the school building, which resulted in further stigmatism and separation from their peers.

Inclusion refocuses the LRE provision to keep a student in the class that he or she would attend if not disabled. Services are provided in the regular classroom unless the nature and severity of the student's individual educational needs are such that a more restrictive setting must be considered for the child to be provided an appropriate education.

An educational debate is ongoing regarding inclusive education of disabled children. This conflict involves two basic groups: parents, teachers, and administrators who support inclusion, and representatives of these groups who are against inclusion as an educational philosophy and practice.

Inclusion is presented as a generalization that is interpreted by many people as meaning all children with disabilities must be taught in a regular classroom. At one end of the spectrum, proponents of inclusive education are parents and teachers of disabled students who want all children educated in their neighborhood school, with support services provided to the students in the regular classroom. Some educators believe that inclusion will end labeling, special education, and special classes but will not eliminate the necessary supports and services required by children in the regular classroom (Pearpoint & Forest, 1992). Contrarily, parents and teachers of nondisabled children and some disabled children perceive an inability to meet the needs of disabled students in the regular classroom.

Parents and teachers of disabled and nondisabled students have verbalized strong opinions for and against inclusive practices. Parents of disabled students are fearful that services for students, for which they have fought hard since the 1970s, would not be available under inclusion. Segregated school sites for some students are perceived as a safe haven by parents, providing all of the services that their children need.

Parents of nondisabled students fear that their children would be neglected in the classroom because of the significant needs of disabled students. Schools have limited resources, and many programs have been cut because of a lack of funds. Parents are concerned that if resources in the regular classroom are geared to the disabled students, fewer resources and less support will be available to the nondisabled students.

Survey results compiled by the New York State Commission on Quality of Care for the Mentally Disabled (Sundram, 1990) indicated that 64% of the parents of disabled children were satisfied with the educational placement of their children, and the children were equally represented among segregated sites, special education classes, and regular classrooms. Parents who were satisfied with their children's programs expressed concern about change.

Special education teachers are fearful that positions will be cut. Classroom teachers fear not being able to teach students with whom they have not been trained to deal in their classroom, as well as a lack of support from school administration, other teachers, and paraprofessionals.

School administrators also have expressed concern about inclusive practices. Special education administrators are concerned about compliance with IDEA's LRE clause and want to ensure that a full continuum of services exists for children found eligible for services as disabled students. Building principals are concerned about how to manage the schedules of teachers, students, and program components within budgetary constraints. Class size is growing, resources are limited, and the management of an ever-changing, diverse student body needs attention.

The inclusion movement has redefined mainstreaming, which has been the LRE interpretation of IDEA. The location of services for an eligible student is determined by considering the regular classroom with support for the teacher and student first before removing a student from a class for separate special education services. The continuum includes part-time support in or out of the regular classroom, full-time support in special classes in district schools, special schools, and residential settings.

Since 1975, the criteria by which students with a disability are found eligible for services, class size, frequency of services, and an individual educational plan (IEP) have been required by mandates to ensure an appropriate education for disabled students. The committee must consider the LRE, but the full continuum of services still exists now as it has since the implementation of P.L. 94-142 in 1975.

Between 1990 and 1994, many regular school programs have been cut for budgetary reasons, whereas special education programs have expanded because of compliance issues with mandates. Ironically, although districts must comply with regulations to receive federal funds, the federal funds provide only 5% to 8% of the funds necessary to run the mandated programs. When these programs were initiated, 40% of the funds were supposed to be federally funded.

Teacher unions issued statements regarding inclusion. The official position of the unions was that teachers should not be forced to be involved with inclusive programs because of lack of training, funds, and interest. The American Federation of Teachers (AFT) president, Albert Shanker, wrote three articles that were published in the *New York Times* in 1994, and he spoke on inclusion at the AFT conference in Washington DC, initiating a moratorium on inclusion (*Early Childhood Report*, 1994). He warned members against the placement of all disabled students in regular classrooms without the regulations being followed. The AFT requested that policymakers (a) balance the needs of all students in schools and that consideration be given to the federal government's funding of 40% of special education, as originally planned in 1975; (b) give teachers the right to provide input in determining which students should be placed in regular classes; (c) give teachers the right to appeal eligibility decisions; (d) provide federal, state, and local funding for supplemental supports for included children; and (e) limit the number of special needs children in regular classrooms. A major concern involved the pendency rule of the regulations, which entitles a student to stay in a program while a placement is being challenged. Students with significant behavioral needs are a concern of teachers, and pendency rules for these students have been questioned by the AFT.

As noted in the 15th Annual Report to Congress (U.S. Department of Education, 1993a), 94.4% of students receiving services in special education attend regular school. Of those students, 69.3% spend more than 40% of their school day in the general classroom (Ayers, 1994). Inclusion is not a new mandate, as this data supports.

Inclusion reminds educators of the need to provide services for identified students in the least restrictive environment.

The concerns of the teachers are real. However, the AFT does not realize that many of its concerns are addressed in the current regulations, because school district implementation of the regulations vastly differs. Teachers *should* play a role in the eligibility process, and the child's current classroom teacher *should* be a member of the eligibility committee. Inclusion does not mean that every disabled child must be educated in a regular classroom. If decisions are made on an individual basis, a student with severe behavioral needs may be determined to need the structure of a small class, with a low student-teacher ratio, in order to receive an appropriate education. The point of LRE is to ensure that the individual rights of each disabled student are considered when planning an appropriate educational program, rather than placing all students in a particular program, in a particular location, because of an assigned label.

On a national level, 66% of all disabled students, K-12, have been classified as either learning disabled or speech impaired between the 1982-1983 and 1990-1991 school years (U.S. Department of Education, 1994). In 1990-1991, 2,130,000 students were found eligible for services as learning disabled students. By definition, learning disabled students have, at minimum, an average intellectual ability, with processing deficits affecting the students' achievement levels and resulting in a lack of congruency with ability levels. These students had different abilities, strengths, and weaknesses and needed placements in school ranging in support from a resource teacher to maintain grade-level skills to a full-time placement out of the regular class in order to provide the resources necessary to enable students to learn. The differences between students identified as learning disabled at the elementary level and the general population in terms of behaviors and skills are minimal (Oakland, Shermis, & Coleman, 1990).

How Inclusion Practices Vary Among States and Districts

Inclusion places the focus on the LRE provision for school eligibility committees, including parents, to look at each child's ability; to consider what a child can gain in the areas of academic, social/emotional, physical, and/or behavior/management areas as a member of the regular class; and to determine how to support the child so that learning can take place. Each of these areas is considered separately and together, as academics alone do not educate any child. Only if a child cannot learn in the regular classroom can the eligibility committee look for a more restrictive setting for portions of the school day. Children who are eligible for services under the requirements of IDEA exhibit a wide range of disabling conditions, with varied learning needs.

The LRE provision was intended to focus on the regular classroom with support services as a *first* step in determining a student's appropriate education. After this consideration, more restrictive settings, such as pull-out classes or alternative school settings, would be considered the least restrictive setting for an individual student's educational program.

IDEA contains a due process clause, which enables parents to challenge the eligibility, disabling condition, or services provided in the educational plan for their child. A parent has the right to ask for an impartial hearing, and the district must act upon this request within 10 days. The parents do not have to pay for an impartial hearing, which costs a school district an average of $50,000. If the parents choose to hire an attorney, they would be reimbursed for costs if they win or if they prove to the hearing officer that the complaint was a legitimate one, even if the case was won by the school district. The student remains in the current placement, the last agreed-upon program, during any hearing or court challenges unless the parent or guardian agrees to a change in program while the proceedings take place.

Inclusion is a refocusing of the LRE provision, but different professionals and politicians define inclusion differently. For example, Syracuse University has led a training program that focused on total inclusion for severely disabled students, as a way of enabling all children to be part of a socialized group in their neighborhood school. A statewide grant provided funding for this project, and a requirement of this grant was to train school district personnel in New York State to apply full inclusion in their schools. This is an example of one philosophical descriptor of inclusion.

Another version of inclusion is the involvement of a student with significant, multiple handicaps being educated in a typical classroom setting. Districts have described a wheelchair-bound student receiving services in a regular class as inclusion, whereas other districts have been including wheelchair-bound students in classes since 1975.

It is important to note that what is deemed a "new inclusive program" in one district may not be considered inclusion in another, where it is common, historical practice.

Some schools include all children with all disabilities in the regular classroom. This scenario results in complaints of "dumping" children into one setting without proper preparation or regard for individual student needs.

One of President Clinton's televised town meetings in 1993 showed a disabled young girl, confined to a wheelchair because of cerebral palsy, asking him why her twin sister, who was more severely disabled, was not allowed to attend the same school in New York City. He told her that he did not know but would check into the situation. Inclusion automatically became a nationally highlighted issue, referred to in local and national media.

The National Association of School Boards of Education published a report in 1992 that told state school boards that they must take steps to ensure that disabled students are taught with nondisabled peers (Viadero, 1992). This led states to create LRE statements and plans as the debate about inclusive practices focused on fiscal implications, personnel, and Goals 2000 outcomes. In the National Education Goals Report (U.S. Department of Education, 1993b), an emphasis is placed on quality education for all children. The report reflects a nationwide philosophical belief that consensus on desired changes in education will provide a way for educators to move toward outcomes desired for all children in American schools.

The Learning Disabilities Association of America (LDA), one of the largest disability advocacy groups, wanted states to think and move slowly in changing the delivery of special education services. They stated concerns about disabled students' being taught in regular classrooms "if that happens to be the best place for them" (*Special Education Report*, 1993). The regulations state that an *appropriate* education, in the least restrictive setting, be determined based on the individual needs of a student. The regulations never intended to propose that the best education possible be provided, but an adequate one, as delineated in the Rowley decision in chapter 2.

The Council for Exceptional Children (CEC) published a statement in the spring of 1993 of support for full inclusion. This was defined as "the effective and supported inclusion of students with disabilities with their nonhandicapped peers" (Viadero, 1993, p. 5). CEC further stated that schools would be places where the building administrator and staff members would be responsible for all students receiving education in the building. This necessitates a change to the belief that disabled children in the building are part of the responsibility of the entire building staff, not solely of special education teachers or departments using space for "their" children in a building.

In 1986, the assistant secretary of education published a report calling for more cooperation between special education and regular education in combining children with learning problems into regular classrooms (Dawson, 1987). Concerns stated in the report included:

- There was a fragmented approach to providing students with identified disabilities services based on criteria that enabled some children to fall through the cracks because they were not eligible for services.
- Children were grouped by labels, rather than individual needs.
- Schools were given fiscal incentives to place children in programs for a majority of the school day.

Madeline Will (1987) challenged educators to "take what we have learned from the special programs and begin to transfer this knowledge to the regular classroom" (p. 1). A call to place less emphasis on labels and more on teaching individual students with learning problems was widely discussed in the late 1980s. This was the "regular education initiative," which was supposed to encourage partnerships between special and regular education to investigate ways to serve students with mild and moderate disabilities in the regular classroom. However, until inclusion was perceived as a mandate, policymakers and educators did little to change the delivery of services or combine professional philosophies between special education and regular education, as defined under LRE.

Funding Special Education Programs: New Approaches

Funding issues will arise because funding mechanisms for supporting special education services are a concern of many educators. Special education funds are distributed in most states based on the number of children identified as having a specific disability, as well as hours spent receiving special education services. This system is dependent on labeling and categorization. States are beginning to change traditional funding methodology not as a result of inclusive practices, but in ways that will support inclusive practices. For example, the state of Vermont has a new funding formula that allows for a unified system of education. Block grants are awarded to each district to cover basic costs of special education services, based on previous year enrollments and state average salaries of mainstream special educators. South Carolina has redistributed funds in ways that allow for a unified system, and New York is looking at ways of changing funding by 1996.

The formula that provides state funds derived by a head count of students with disabilities is being challenged. This method versus population-based funding, where states receive funds according to a census of all students aged 3 to 21, is being investigated by the Department of Education. Support for change is evident, but consensus of how and when to change has not been reached. Some states, including Vermont, Massachusetts, Pennsylvania, and Montana, have already adopted population-based funding. Concern from other states revolves around the possibility of switching to a population-based method, which may result in large shifts of money allocated for students with disabilities, penalize some states whose management of identification and service procedures is significantly different from other states where rules have been more lax, and lead to underidentification of students with true disabilities. Some authorities believe that financial incentives to identify disabled students are no longer necessary because the initial implementation of IDEA to ensure a free and appropriate education to students with disabilities is understood and IDEA is fully implemented. These proponents of change believe that this head-count funding mechanism has led to the overidentification of students with disabilities.

The CEC has stated that the funding questions should be addressed separately from the reauthorization of IDEA in 1995 (CEC, 1995). Reviews of reports from the Office of Special Education Programs indicates similar concerns. Unless there was a transition period, states with greater numbers of students with disabilities would lose funds by changing to a population-based funding system. Additionally, fiscal accountability and maintenance of appropriate levels of funding could be jeopardized, which in turn might negate program components for disabled students. If disabled students were not appropriately identified and funds were used for other school programs, the right of a free, appropriate education to disabled students would be abdicated.

Avoiding Inclusion Confusion

Many districts jumped into the perceived new program philosophy of inclusion and now must address issues that would not exist if implementation of inclusive programs initially followed an intervention strategy. If administrators in the school do not understand the educational objectives of inclusive education, support is minimized, the self-worth of the participants in the school is negated, and confusion evolves. Fear, anger, and mistrust then guide actions rather than a development of necessary resources that would help staff, parents, and the students. The collaboration and involvement of all professionals in school systems and a change in philosophy of administrators are vital components of improving the education of students.

The language of educators must focus on common terms so that discussions between educators, parents, students, and community members can take place. This book focuses on educating all children in a caring environment that administrators, parents, teachers, and community members can support.

Children in schools reflect a broad spectrum of diversity. The more educators separate and label students by programs, services, or disability, the further split the educational community becomes. The educational needs of children need to be addressed as societal issues in today's world, not as separate molecules of nonrelated matter. Limited resources require educators to compete for student programs, delineating support of the educational community by parents, teachers, community members, and taxpayers. Professionals and parents do not want to choose which students' needs are more worthy, and each group wants to protect its interests, support students, and allow children to benefit from their educational experience. Special education is *not* a place. It is the provision of support services to help students learn!

2

Complying With IDEA:
Legal Issues in Special Education

Legal Background and Overview

The courts have been involved in educational issues since the U.S. Constitution mandated that states have plenary, or final, authority, and education was decentralized so that the people could have control and responsibility for local education. There is an administrative structure in each state under the Department of Education in which due process hearings under the IDEA regulations can be held. An impartial hearing officer is assigned to rule on a dispute involving disagreements regarding children with disabilities. Appeals can be made to the commissioner of education, or state boards of education, depending on the state structure. The decisions of the state's final appeal process can be challenged in federal court. There are 12 judicial circuits in the country, including the District of Columbia, and each has a district court where an issue is first challenged. There is the Circuit Court of Appeals, where district court rulings are brought to trial, and if two or more circuit courts conflict, the U.S. Supreme Court may rule on a case. The decisions of the district or circuit court become laws within that court's jurisdiction. The Supreme Court ruling becomes the law of the land.

The court cases that led to the inclusion movement will be described in this chapter in chronological order. In 1954, the *Brown v. Board of Education* decision set the standard that separate education is not equal education. Separation of educational programs can

> generate a feeling of inferiority as to [children's] status in the community that may affect their hearts and minds in a way unlikely ever to be undone. This sense of inferiority . . . affects the motivation of a child to learn . . . [and] has a tendency to retard . . . educational and mental development. (Chief Justice Earl Warren, *Brown v. Board of Education*, 1954)

This decision was the basis used by parents and advocates of the disabled in challenging the exclusion and segregation of children with disabilities in *Wyatt v. Stickney* (1971), *Pennsylvania Association for Retarded Citizens v. Commonwealth of Pennsylvania* (1972), and in *Mills v. Board of Education* (1972). The Mills decision stated that merely placing a child in a regular class or special class was not enough. Support and ancillary services in regular education were preferable over placement in a special class.

In 1973, the Office of Civil Rights (OCR) amended its policies to include Section 504 of the Rehabilitation Act (1973), which added disabilities to the OCR entitlements. Senator Hubert Humphrey, whose granddaughter had Down's syndrome, supported this bill, which ensured that students with disabilities had equal protection under the law. Section 504 of the Rehabilitation Act relating to elementary, middle, and secondary education provides that no individual with handicaps "shall, solely by reason of her or his handicap, be excluded from participation in, be denied the benefits of, or be subjected to discrimination under any program or activity receiving Federal financial assistance." The definition of a handicapped or disabled person under the Rehabilitation Act is broader than the definition under IDEA. A disabled person includes anyone who "has a physical or mental impairment which substantially limits one or more major life activities, has a record of such an impairment, or is regarded as having such an impairment."

The Education for All Handicapped Children Act of 1975, P.L. 94-142, and its amendment, the Education of the Handicapped Act, P.L. 99-457 (1986), created a law that entitled children with disabilities, aged 3 to 21, to a free, appropriate education in the least restrictive environment. This law was renamed the Individuals with Disabilities Education Act in 1990. Section 504 of the Rehabilitation Act differs from IDEA in that identified students need special education and related services. Children identified under 504 are entitled to accommodations deemed necessary to ensure access to all public school programs and activities, but may not need special education and related services. All children identified with disabilities under IDEA are also protected under 504, but all children covered under 504 are not necessarily students with a disability under IDEA.

In the early 1980s, court decisions focused on schools providing children with an appropriate education, with LRE being a secondary consideration (*Board of Education of East Windsor v. Diamond*, 1986; *Johnston v. Ann Arbor Public Schools*, 1983; *Wilson v. Marana Unified School District*, 1984). As long as an appropriate education was being provided, one from which a child could benefit educationally, the courts supported placement in segregated settings.

In 1983, *Roncker v. Walter* in the Sixth Circuit Court of Appeals ruled on a challenge in the Ohio school's system regarding the placement of all severely retarded students into segregated schools operated by the county. The parents of a 9-year-old boy did not think that the segregated school, which offered no interaction with nondisabled peers, was the least restrictive environment for their son. The circuit court agreed, and in its ruling stated that placements needed to be made on an individual basis, rather than on the categorical labeling of disabled students. This was one of the first decisions to determine that a balance between academic and socialization needs should be looked at before determining an LRE placement for a student as an appropriate educational setting.

There have been numerous challenges of the law (P.L. 94-142/IDEA) since its inception. In 1982, the U.S. Supreme Court heard the *Board of Education of Hendrick Hudson Central School District v. Rowley* case. This decision mandated that the appropriateness of a proposed placement be determined by whether or not the placement "is reasonably calculated to enable the child to receive educational benefits." According to the court, the Education for All Handicapped Children Act (1975) does not require states to maximize the potential of each disabled child.

Discipline Decisions

As part of inclusion confusion, the discipline available for students with disabilities has been interpreted by some educators to mean that a disabled student who becomes a danger to him- or herself or others cannot be suspended or removed from school. This is not correct, and this issue needs to be clarified because fearful concern of professionals and community members is growing under perceived inclusion mandates.

In 1988, a U.S. Supreme Court decision, *Honig v. Doe,* restricted a school's ability to unilaterally suspend or expel a disabled student from class. School discipline is a major issue in the 1990s because weapons use and availability pose a threat to school safety.

In the Honig decision, Chief Justice Brennan stated "that Congress (P.L. 94-142) . . . meant to strip schools of the *unilateral* authority they had traditionally employed to exclude disabled students, particularly emotionally disturbed students, from school." He further stated that the law "directed that in the future the removal of disabled students could be accomplished only with the permission of the parents or, as a last resort, the courts." In court, officials can overcome the "stay put" or pendency presumption by showing that the student is likely to harm him- or herself or others. The school district is responsible for having an eligibility meeting to determine if a child's disability is the cause of the action that precipitated the suspension. If it is, the district must decide whether a different placement is warranted, so that the student can be provided an appropriate education. If the placement is changed, all disciplinary actions are dropped and arrangements are made to provide instruction in a different setting. If the eligibility committee decides the action and the student's disability have no causal relationship, disciplinary actions continue, consistent with rules applicable to any student. Although this has been interpreted to mean that a continuity of educational services still must be provided under IDEA, challenges have begun to surface. In *Metropolitan School District of Wayne Township v. Davilla* (1991), the Southern School District of Indiana filed a class action suit against the assistant secretary of the U.S. Department of Education at the Office of Special Education and Rehabilitation Services. The secretary sent a policy letter stating that the school district had to provide an education to suspended and expelled students, even when the behavior that prompted the disciplinary action was found not to be related to the student's disability. The school district disagreed and claimed that the information in the secretary's letter was in conflict with current case law interpreting IDEA. The court's findings supported the school district, referring to *Honig v. Doe,* and stated that if a disabled student was suspended or expelled properly and if there was found no causal relationship between the student's action and his or her disability, the school did not have to provide educational services. Additionally, the federal court distinguished the fact that in the Honig decision, the U.S. Supreme Court only dealt with the situation of disciplining students whose disability had a causal relationship with disciplinary actions.

Discipline of disabled students continues to be a major issue in the 1990s because school safety is a national concern. The laws governing the disciplinary actions of disabled students must be followed, but it is important to note that students who pose a threat to themselves or others can be taken out of the school setting, through either parental agreement or injunctive relief through the courts.

Changes in LRE Consideration

State and federal courts as well as the U.S. Supreme Court have ruled on various aspects of IDEA. In 1989, in *Daniel R. R. v. State Board of Education,* the court held that a separate class for a student with Down's syndrome, classified as mentally retarded, was appropriate. The court's decision stated that students with severe disabilities may be placed in segregated classes when they cannot be satisfactorily educated in a general education setting. This decision created a two-step test of LRE for determining when a school district met its obligation to include children with severe disabilities in regular classrooms. The appeals court stated that school districts must first determine if a child can be educated satisfactorily in the regular classroom with supplemental aids or services. If students could not benefit from education in a regular class with support, those receiving special education services outside of the regular classroom had to be mainstreamed to the maximum extent possible. To evaluate the two-step test of LRE, the disabled student's ability to grasp the regular education curriculum, the nature and severity of the disability, the effect the disabled student's presence would have on the functioning of the regular classroom unit, and the amount of time that the disabled student would spend with nondisabled peers had to be considered.

Inclusion of students with disabilities was measured against the two-step test of LRE that the Fifth Circuit's ruling provided.

The U.S. Court of Appeals, Third Circuit (New Jersey), also ruled on an inclusion case. In *Oberti v. Board of Education of Clementon School District* (1993), the parents of an 8-year-old child with Down's syndrome sought full inclusion for their son in a regular classroom. The school district had placed this elementary-school-aged student in a self-contained, special education classroom. A federal judge determined that the school district did not follow the LRE clause of IDEA and did not prove that the child was incapable of being integrated into the regular classroom. The school district was ordered to include the child in a regular class.

The court's decision stated that to determine whether a child with disabilities can be educated in a regular class with supportive services, the following three factors must be considered: (a) whether the school district made reasonable efforts to accommodate the child in the regular classroom with supplemental aides and services, (b) the educational benefits available to the child in the regular classroom, and (c) the possible negative effects on other students in the class. The court noted that a special education placement cannot be justified by the fact that a child may make more academic progress in a self-contained, special education class.

Benefit Factors

The *Oberti* case (1993) reaffirmed the intent of IDEA and reemphasized the need for all four areas covered by an individual education plan (academic, social/emotional, behavioral, and physical) to be equally considered by eligibility committees in determining an appropriate school placement for a child. Additionally, the court stated that a comparison between the educational benefits that a child would receive in a regular classroom with support versus the benefits that the child would receive in a segregated classroom must be looked at when determining an inclusive placement. Focus was placed on socialization and communication, as well as improved self-esteem benefits, not only academic or educational benefits, which were the standards used in determining mainstream program components during the 1970s and 1980s. This reaffirmed the fundamental right of students with disabilities to receive a public education with nondisabled peers.

The recognition that a disabled child can benefit differently from education than other students is a significant acknowledgment that stems from the ruling in *Daniel R. R.*, which specifies that this difference alone does not justify exclusion from the regular classroom.

The other significant factor discussed in the court focused on the negative impact on other students in the classroom of placing a disabled child into the setting. This was explained in the ruling to mean that if a disabled child merely requires more teacher attention than most other children, this was not a negative effect. If, however, a child was so disruptive that he or she significantly impaired the ability of other children to learn, this would be a negative effect requiring that the school district look for placement of the disabled child for all or part of the school day in a small special education class.

The burden of proof that the full continuum of services, based on LRE, is looked at in the placement of each disabled child is the responsibility of the school district. The possibilities are individually determined, and time spent with nondisabled peers needs to be maximized.

The U.S. Court of Appeals, Ninth Circuit (California), 1994, ordered a school district to place a disabled child in a regular second-grade classroom (*Sacramento City Unified School District v. Holland*, 1992). The school district urged the court to adopt a test for evaluating compliance with IDEA's mainstreaming requirement that centers on the category of a child's disability. The court found that because the purpose of IDEA is based on individual children's needs, this was not possible. The court restated that placement decisions must be made based on a child's individual needs and abilities, not a label or category.

Financial Considerations

The Sacramento City Unified School District also raised the issue of cost consideration for a placement decision. The district contended that because the state department of education assigns more funds to the cost per pupil for educating a disabled child, based on time spent in special education classes, it would be significantly more expensive to the district to educate a disabled child in the regular classroom. The court disagreed. The court said that to make an appropriate comparison, the district would need to compare "the cost of placing Rachel in a special class with a full-time special education teacher and two full-time aides with approximately 11 other children, . . . and the cost of placing her in a regular class with a part-time aide" (*Sacramento City Unified School District v. Holland*, 1992).

In this decision, the court referred to another case involving the cost of educating disabled children, *Greer v. Rome City School District* (1992), in which the Eleventh Circuit Court wrote that "if the cost of educating a handicapped child in a regular classroom is so great that it would significantly impact upon the education of other children in the district, then education in a regular class is not appropriate." However, a specification of the financial cost difference that would be considered significant was not determined in either this case or in the Holland decision.

The Holland decision did add cost consideration as a fourth factor to the Oberti decision's three-step test. The four-part test was set forth as precedent to be used to determine if a disabled student's placement meets the LRE requirement under IDEA. The Sacramento City Unified School District's appeal to the U.S. Supreme Court to hear the Holland case was declined. Legally, inclusive education was defined for schools as of this ruling.

Compliance Issues

Schools must comply with the federal regulations regarding educating disabled students. The laws allow for students with varying degrees of disabilities to be placed in an assortment of educational programs based on individual needs and the LRE. It is imperative that educators and parents understand that the LRE for one child may be the regular classroom, but for another child, the LRE may be a residential school. The full continuum of services still exists because inclusion has not changed the law; rather, inclusion has reemphasized a part of the law. Correct information about the regulations must be communicated consistently to the educational community so that students, teachers, administrators, and parents become knowledgeable and able to support all students' educational programs.

In Loudoun County, Virginia, a due process hearing was initiated involving inclusion. This case was unusual because the school district initiated the hearing in order to remove a student with autism and significant behavioral problems from a fully inclusive placement in a second-grade classroom. The media (*Washington Post*, PBS) got involved because the parents requested that the hearing process be open.

The student, Mark Hartmann, attended an inclusive first-grade class in Illinois with the support of a full-time aide, and he used facilitated communication as a mechanism for communicating. The prior school reported that Mark was able to read, follow the class routine, and interact with nondisabled peers. Loudoun County hired an aide to work with Mark and trained staff in facilitated communication, and the classroom teacher was trained in inclusive practices. The district believed it had prepared well for Mark in continuing his prior placement according to school reports and parental requests.

By February of his second-grade year, the teacher and aide questioned Mark's ability in skills as well as his interaction with peers. They stated that the only interacting he did involved physically aggressive actions toward others, including pinching, biting, and hitting. The staff also reported that Mark was not able to read or follow class routines, and appeared to be unaware of his environment. He also had frequent episodes of making squealing noises that the teacher tried to ignore, and he exhibited very distracting behaviors that disrupted the educational setting for all other students in the class.

The district recommended placing Mark in a program for children with autism, which was located in another regular school, and including him for part of the school day. He would attend nonacademic subjects with nondisabled peers. His parents acknowledged the lack of learning for Mark and the disruption to the class but wanted him in a fully inclusive setting so that socialization would be maximized. The district then requested a hearing.

On December 15, 1994, the hearing officer found that the Loudoun County School District could remove Mark from the regular third-grade class he was attending and send him to another regular school 10 miles away. There, he could attend a program for children with autism and be included for nonacademic subjects. In the decision, the hearing officer stated that although Mark's parents claimed the school district had not provided enough training to Mark's aide and teacher, the Loudoun school system had made a "substantial effort" to assist Mark in an attempt to have him succeed in the regular classroom. The hearing officer pointed out that the school had assigned a smaller number of students to his class (21 instead of 26) and that his classmates were children who were least likely to need extra attention.

After the decision was announced, the superintendent of schools in Loudoun County stressed that this case should not be interpreted as a setback for disabled children. He reiterated the need for decisions to be made on an individual student basis and stated that "this has been a case about one student's education, not about inclusion in general" (Pae, 1994).

The most important considerations of school districts in recommending placement options for students with disabilities are ensuring that procedural due process is followed, that parents are partners in the eligibility process, and that the four-step plan for determining the LRE is followed. This will allow for the full continuum of services to be available to students on an individual basis, provide documentation of need for inclusive or more restrictive settings when appropriate, and allow parents to be partners in planning their child's educational goals.

3

Planning Inclusive Programs in Your School

Determining Goals and Roles of Personnel

Educating all students, regardless of disabling condition, in their neighborhood school is the goal of inclusive education. A strong sense of community in the classroom, throughout the school, and among parents of all students is necessary for an inclusive program (Davern, 1992). A flexible curriculum and support for staff and students are necessary components of an inclusive model.

Establishing school-based plans for educating children with disabling conditions in the regular classroom setting is a shared responsibility of regular and special educators (Jenkins, Jewell, Leicester, Jenkins, & Troutner, 1991; Nowacek, 1992). An inclusion model requires general educators to assume a greater responsibility for educating students with disabling conditions, and roles of teachers and paraprofessionals need to be clarified.

The educational community recognizes the need for restructuring programs, the delivery of support services, and home-school partnerships, and the need to restructure schools to encompass these goals in order to assist children in developing social skills (Buswell &

Schaffner, 1992; Cronin, Slade, Bechtel, & Anderson, 1992; Hogges & Spiva, 1993). Disabled and nondisabled children all need a sense of belonging and to feel valued as members of their schools and communities. Inclusion of students in their neighborhood schools, with supportive services brought to the students, can be an effective educational model.

Inclusive education requires a restructuring of how services are delivered to children, and a focused effort for "push-in" rather than "pull-out" services is the key. Parents' awareness of regulatory change enhances the roles of the students, school personnel, and home. This partnership supports a plan for educational change (Cordisco & Laus, 1993).

Collaboration of regular and special education teachers naturally occurs as children with special needs spend more time in regular education. Consultant services develop into a support system for professionals in the school in order to help students succeed in the classroom. Collaborative efforts should focus on shared concerns that could be worked on in school and at home so that parents are partners in their children's education. Collaboration is a crucial component for improvement of educational services to students with special needs.

Giving teachers control of a classroom, policy, and programs is a useful tool in support of collaboration. Effective education collaboration needs to focus on shared responsibilities, mutual respect, joint planning, reciprocal support, a common educational philosophy, and systemic evaluation and dissemination of information.

Current Practices

Inclusion programs have been unsuccessful for the following reasons:

- Little or no training for teachers
- Quick, fearful response by schools to outside pressures
- Lack of understanding by parents and professionals of what inclusion should be
- Small initiative for one child by two cooperating teachers with no plans for follow-through for subsequent years
- Lack of central office, board of education, and administrative support

For example, educational leaders in Palm Beach County, Florida, believed that inclusion meant that all disabled students had to be taught in neighborhood schools, in regular classrooms. Their mission statement indicates that "all individuals with exceptionalities will successfully achieve full inclusion within their community," and 100% of "exceptional students will achieve 100% of their personal goals." Even though other parts of their mission statement and references to a joint philosophy statement regarding inclusion in the state of Florida refer to other objectives regarding the least restrictive environment (LRE) regulations and a continuum of services for students with exceptionalities, conflicting statements were noted. The joint statement specifies that Florida's inclusion initiative is intended to "enhance the mandate for education in the LRE, so that inclusion means less exclusion and more inclusionary educational environments are provided." Any local policy statement that all exceptional students will be included leads to concern for the eligibility process and subsequent development of individual education plan (IEP) goals and objectives for individual students. It is important that a policy statement, intended to meet one aspect of the educational community's plan, does not conflict with other statements, causing concern and confusion.

Support for students with exceptionalities is directed toward staff training, monetary support, methodology, and inclusion for all students in Palm Beach County's inclusion policy. However, as of September 1993, teachers in one school reported that students were placed into their classes based on the philosophy of full inclusion with little or no teacher training and no parental communication for parents of disabled or nondisabled students, and chaos ensued. Forty percent of the inclusion class in each elementary grade were students identified with disabilities. Both regular and special education teachers reported dissatisfaction with inclusive classrooms. Teachers had no time to prepare for a combined class of children with diverse needs, where more than one teacher shared responsibility for the education of some of the students, and teachers complained about a lack of information about students with disabilities placed in their classrooms.

Similarly, in Howard County, Maryland, inclusion became an issue in 1993, when students were placed in their neighborhood schools, with little or no teacher training and a lack of communication with staff, administration, or parents of nondisabled students. Teachers at the junior high level and parents at the elementary and junior high level shared information, indicating the lack of communication of program changes. Parents reported that severely disabled students shared a learning environment with nondisabled classes, and no one discussed the change in program location or program goals with parents of the nondisabled students. Parents did not express concern about including disabled students but were dissatisfied that no one told them about the changes in the school.

The Restructuring Process

A system of change must have a focused plan, contain mechanisms for communication with and among all component parts, and establish a shared mission or goal. Restructuring schools by merging aspects of special education and regular education allows students with mild disabilities to strengthen abilities, encourages educators to work together rather than provide a fragmented approach for students, and strengthens the skills of underachievers in the classroom without disabilities (Fuchs & Fuchs, 1994). The ability of administrators to recognize that change takes time—that staff members need to research and explore topics, and share information and concerns in a nonthreatening atmosphere in order to be partners in change—is vital to inclusive education. Once staff members recognize the educational worth of change, excitement and creativity begin to drive the change process. Once a few staff members feel positive about educational change, colleagues begin to jump on the proverbial bandwagon. The continuance of change and the ability of staff members to have input into the change process encourages innovative practices from which children, teachers, parents, and administrators benefit.

Change in an organization can be threatening, exciting, or ignored by staff, depending on how change is structured. In schools, change encompasses three main areas: curricular, self-improvement of staff, and schoolwide linkages for enhanced student learning. The health of an organization involves the dimensions of goal focus, communication adequacy, morale, innovation, resource utilization, autonomy, flexibility, and the ability to solve problems (Miles, 1965). Restructuring efforts can and should focus upon these factors. Educational restructuring that creates a unified system also provides all children a nurturing environment in which to learn, based on individual strengths and weaknesses, regardless of labels. Site-based management, shared expectations of all students by all staff members, and district support for staff training allow schools to develop a unified system of educating children.

Time is critical to all members of the school community. Teachers should have the opportunity to gain information and knowledge from each other. The need for a school's faculty to meet together to discuss educational practices is not negated once teachers are trained in a new program, nor when the program is implemented (Raywid, 1993). The decisions of how to incorporate these practices in the classroom should be made by shared decision making and bottom-up planning with the staff of each building. A districtwide mission should be established and followed by each school, but in ways unique to each school's culture.

The culture of each school is different. The establishment of a balance between the general milieu of the school and the influence of how teachers view the school in relation to their ability to be supported and be innovative in the classroom is crucial (Hopkins, 1990). A building-based model of decision making to plan inclusive practices is vital to ensure program success.

This team approach incorporates all stakeholders in the school as members of the planning team. The value of the team approach supports the fact that representatives from many disciplines can make better decisions concerning the education of children (Courtnage & Smith-Davis, 1987). Teachers need to be trained to be team players because teaching is an isolated practice. Teachers are traditionally the sole proprietors of the instructional process in their classrooms (Lortie, 1975). New teachers need support from experienced colleagues, and experienced teachers need to be exposed to current educational practices.

Implementing Structural Change

Parents, administrators, and teachers need to be part of student-centered planning teams. A team-based model will reflect a holistic approach to learning for all students, and decisions will become more child centered. Team teaching, shared planning, and an outcomes-based model provide a framework for student success. Team teaching or coteaching between regular and special educators is most supportive to children with identified disabling conditions, as well as all other children in the classroom, who benefit from having two teachers in the room for all or part of the school day (Friend & Cook, 1992).

A project plan needs to be developed and implemented when planning inclusive programs in your school. Accurate information needs to be disseminated. Teachers, parents, administrators, and students need to be included in all stages of developing and actualizing a change in the delivery of services for some students. Staff inservice training, staff and parent input, and pilot program implementation should be focused on as facilitators of this process, both at the district and school level.

A planned staff development program is crucial to the success of structural change. Staff inservice training allows participants to gain and share information, pose questions, work collaboratively toward solutions, and learn about new techniques and strategies. An evaluation or assessment component should be created as part of an ongoing cycle of growth and development.

As professionals explore ways of coordinating efforts to teach shared students, all educators in the school need to gain an understanding about how disabled and nondisabled children learn. Acceptance of responsibility for teaching a larger part of the traditional student body is required of all teachers. Staff development programs need to focus on a common agenda, recognizing that different professionals will play differing roles within that framework. Some teachers will develop their own expertise and then share knowledge with colleagues. Some teachers will review assessment components, and some teachers will be minimally involved.

Creating Parent-School Partnerships

Parents are a crucial component to educational change. Fostering their understanding is necessary to ensure positive communication between home and school. Parents of both disabled and nondisabled children need to understand inclusive education as a positive component of their child's education. Parents need to be made aware of school philosophy changes, and administrators can support teachers and students by hosting information-sharing forums. These can be part of a parent-teacher organization agenda or monthly parent meetings during the school day. It is important to host face-to-face forums in addition to written correspondence through newsletters to parents. This supports building respect for home-school coordination, and if people feel respected, they will share concerns and information. People need to know that they have a right to disagree without fear of repercussion. Parents often think that if they disagree with the teacher or principal, their child will suffer in some way. Parents thus share concerns in the community forums rather than with school personnel. It is important that this conceptual understanding be changed so that parents and school staff can work together in supporting children in their acquisition of knowledge. Creating ways to build mutual respect will assist parents, teachers, and administrators in achieving better communication without values being challenged.

Implementing Inclusion Programs

To successfully begin inclusion programs in a school, a districtwide task force should be formed that is composed of teachers and administrators who volunteer to investigate inclusive practices. This task force serves as a shared planning and decision-making body from which goals are generated. Team members should visit other inclusion programs, attend workshops and seminars, and research inclusive programs. This group will become the facilitators of inclusion pilots in each school in the district. By asking for volunteers representing each school and grade level, a team representing concerns from a K-12 perspective will be formed. This team provides mechanisms for sharing information and getting feedback from individual school staffs that can be incorporated into a philosophically based, districtwide program.

It is important to note that inclusive programs will be and should be different from one another and may vary within and between grades and schools because individual student needs vary. The acknowledgment that these differences are a positive part of a districtwide program is significant. Flexibility is a key component to inclusive classrooms.

Teaching strategies for inclusive settings are synonymous with effective teaching strategies used in any area of education. Teachers need to know that they can teach effectively in a supportive school environment. If teachers are supported by colleagues and administrators, they will allow their students flexibility in sharing their knowledge with peers. If teachers do not fear failure when trying new techniques, children will be more willing to try new ways of gaining knowledge.

A Model Inclusion Project

The Monticello Central School District, New York, is located in the lower Catskills, approximately 75 miles northwest of New York City. It is a school district that has an eclectic population, with rural, urban, and suburban characteristics. An inclusive task force began meeting in January 1993, specifically looking at kindergarten through second grades, to develop inclusive pilot programs.

The primary grades were chosen as a starting point because of a developmental early childhood philosophy in the school district. Developmental education allowed children to learn by doing hands-on activities and supported readiness of children through developmental stages. The district had implemented a districtwide program change between 1988 and 1990, where all K-2 teachers had similar classroom setups based on a developmental philosophy.

The implementation of a developmental curriculum sustains the coordination of teaching all young children simultaneously and in one classroom (Mitchell, 1989; Salisbury, 1991). Early intervention is a proven educational process that helps some children remediate concerns early in school, who thus need less special education (Slavin, Karweit, & Wasik, 1993). One benefit of inclusive education for preschool- and kindergarten-aged students is the fact that young children are more apt to play with peers and not focus on the lack of academic skills of others.

Developing Pilot Programs

Volunteers from professional staff (classroom teachers, special education teachers, speech therapists, psychologists, school social workers, district and building administrators) spent 6 months reviewing literature, visiting program sites of inclusive programs, and creating pilot programs for fall 1993 implementation. The task force met during the summer to plan specifics of the pilot programs. The central administration supported program development by providing funding for summer task force members' pay.

School district and building administrators of the three elementary schools involved also committed time to the pilot programs. The support was important because scheduling was affected in the school buildings where the inclusion programs were implemented.

Task Force Recommendations

The task force first recommended that a kindergarten class in one school be team taught by a special education teacher and a kindergarten teacher for 2 hours each day and that speech therapy also be provided to students within the regular classroom for 1 hour each day. These decisions were based on including five students who would have been placed in a self-contained, special education classroom in the past, and teachers made these recommendations to the eligibility committee. All five students had received services as preschool students with disabilities, so there was a lot of information about each child. Teachers, social workers, and psychologists in the school considered the information after conferring with preschool teachers, reviewing reports, and observing the students in the preschool setting. These five students received the same services they would have received in a self-contained classroom, but in a different location—the regular classroom. The IEP reflected no differences compared to students not in an included program because 2 hours of special education services were provided by the special education teacher, and the recommended speech therapy service for each child was administered in the regular classroom.

The second recommendation of the task force was a speech inclusive program for another pilot in the district, with coteaching between a speech therapist and a kindergarten teacher in the classroom, for 1 hour per day. Five mildly disabled students were identified for this program. The goal was for the coteachers to provide all students in the classroom with a positive language experience; students with identified language and articulation problems remained in the classroom with peers while receiving speech and language services.

The task force members proposed a child study model in the third building as a mechanism for building better communication between staff members. This building had undergone changes in administration, and there had been no full-time administrator in the building for a period of months at the end of the 1992-1993 school year. The task force members defined child study as a team of varied professional school personnel who would regularly meet as a resource for teachers to share concerns regarding students with colleagues in order to enhance student learning. This plan proposed a mechanism for input from other teachers to try classroom alternatives prior to making a referral for special education. One problem noted in surveys distributed to school staff in October 1992 was the need for alternatives for students when disabilities were not suspected. No alternatives in school were perceived as available by teachers for students who were having problems in the classroom but were not known to have a disabling condition. It is important to note that some states mandate a child study referral prior to a referral for a suspected disability but that this was not legal in New York. A child study team could meet to discuss the needs of a child, but it was not a mandatory first step, as in, for example, Virginia, New Jersey, or Maryland. Parents or teachers could make a direct referral to the eligibility committee to investigate if a child had a disabling condition and was in need of special education services.

Members of all three pilots were volunteers derived from task force members. The pilot teams in each building initially had scheduled shared planning time, administrative support, and the ability to support children in need of special education services within the classroom.

Parents of the disabled students were told of the plan for the delivery of services in the regular classroom at the eligibility meeting. Programs were planned by the task force members to share information about all three pilot programs at faculty meetings in September and at parent open house night in the fall. A board of education presentation was made by task force members in the fall of 1993. The task force met throughout the year.

Pilot Program Issues

In each building's pilot program, problems and successes were noted. There were problems in coordinating schedules, having enough shared planning time, and philosophical differences of what developmental education in a kindergarten class should involve. There were also frustrations between coteachers, a lack of communication and understanding with colleagues in the building, changes in administrative support resulting from the absence of a principal because of illness, and fear of what these pilots meant to the rest of the faculty. All of these occurred within the first 2 months of the pilot program.

However, by the 3rd and 4th months, although some of these frustrations remained, the beginning of student impact was noted. For example, there was one student in the kindergarten inclusion class who exhibited behavioral concerns. On the 1st day of school, he had to be carried off the bus to his classroom because he was throwing a tantrum. This occurred on a few subsequent school days. One time, the principal called for the special education team teacher to get the child off the bus because he was having another tantrum, and the teacher arrived only to find it was a different, nondisabled student. This fact allowed a negative focus on inclusion from some faculty members to change slightly because the child was not an included child. By December 1993, this child was encouraged by peers to get in line to go to physical education class because the students did not want to leave until he was able to go with the class. This peer pressure was a direct effect of inclusion, and these young children enabled this child to have success with support in the regular classroom. In fact, by the end of the school year, this child was recommended for fewer services as a disabled student.

In the speech inclusion pilot, by May 1994, students working together in the classroom were modeling correct articulation of sounds to peers and encouraging each other to say words and sentences correctly. The children did not know who needed modeling assistance because this practice had become an integral part of their school day. The speech therapist and kindergarten teacher also modeled speech and language skills as integrated parts of lessons throughout the day.

The child study team pilot allowed for staff members to share information and concerns with colleagues. The school staff liked the ability to conference with peers because they perceived that option not to have existed prior to the availability of child study. The ability to communicate concerns with other professionals was reported by survey results (June 1994) to have had an impact on classroom management techniques, created an enhanced understanding of disabilities, and developed the need for a focused effort to plan alternatives for students who were not suspected of having a disability but needed support in school.

The implementation of the pilot programs enabled the task force members to plan program changes with firsthand knowledge. Changes occurred during the school year as well as for the following year. The most important factor expressed by all participants was the need for a sufficient amount of shared planning time. This had been the major problem identified while researching inclusive practices, and it was found to be a major need of professional staff members. The second factor described by task force members was the ability to coteach with professionals who shared developmental values in communication and practice. The door-to-desk planning required at times necessitated the cooperation and collaboration of coteachers. In the kindergarten classroom with five moderately disabled students, this was a frustration throughout the school year, although improvements were accomplished. In the speech inclusion pilot, the coteachers provided a coordinated program for students, and the problem of coteacher differences was worked out successfully during the first few months of program implementation. The ability to meet and plan with teachers of shared students is vital to the success of a coteaching model. There must be time for team teachers to work out differences of opinion in the delivery of activities so that a conflict in the classroom during the activities with students does not occur.

The administrative support was well planned, but the degree of support was not actualized. Illness of administrators, a changeover in central office personnel, and budgetary concerns affected the support provided for pilot programs. For example, one principal was absent for 3 months, during which time recommended changes in the pilot programs that would have affected the operation of the school schedule for those not involved in the pilots could not take place. Two out of three central office administrators were new to the district, and many programs required priority focus. Cutbacks in funds affected the number of paraprofessionals and the ability to afford professional staff members additional planning time.

Outcomes and New Recommendations

Even though many concerns were noted by participants, and all program components did not actualize as intended, the task force grew and additional pilots were planned for the 1994-1995 school year. In April 1994, the task force members met and highlighted the need for program support, planning time, and enhanced program configuration.

Each pilot was suggested to continue, but with modification and expansion. The pilots were expanded to four at the kindergarten level, and two first-grade inclusive classes. Additionally, a third-grade inclusion class was formed in one school, and a fifth-grade inclusion model was formed in another school. All participants involved were volunteers, and the classroom teachers wanted to team teach with the special education teacher for part of the day as a way of reducing the number of children leaving the classroom for services.

In the middle and high school, one section of one class was team taught as the pilots expanded. A sixth-grade study skills class was cotaught by a classroom teacher and a special education teacher, with 25% of students in the class identified as having a disability. In the high school, an introductory business class was team taught by a special education teacher and a business teacher, with 50% of the class identified as students with a disability. The two pilot inclusive classes (1993-1994) led to 10 inclusion pilots for the 1994-1995 school year.

Teachers involved with the inclusion pilots described a better understanding of disabled students as reported by survey results and recommendations for students in first grade. Teachers demonstrated an increased knowledge of strategies and methodologies for teaching a concept in a multisensory way and exhibited the desire to have input into the program recommendations for shared students. Recommendations for students in the piloted programs ranged from dismissal from special education to support in the regular class to support in a special education class. The individual child's needs were identified, and all children were recommended to spend most of their day in the regular classroom. In prior years, before the pilot program, most of these students were recommended to spend very little time mainstreamed in a regular class and most of the day in a special education program.

As a result of the pilot programs, the philosophical understanding of how children learn was changed for some teachers. The staff began realizing that sharing resources benefited themselves and the students.

One of the strongest recommendations from task force participants was to cluster children who receive similar services within the regular education class. Children receiving resource room support should be placed in the regular class in groups of five, rather than one or two students spread in three to five classes. Children receiving direct instruction in math or reading at the elementary level, or speech and language services, should also be clustered into a limited number of classes in each grade. Teachers involved in the pilot programs stated that clustering students allowed for maximum use of team-teaching time, and planning for activities in the classroom was accomplished with more success. By clustering students, all children benefited because grouping students for activities was more successful compared to the common "airport" feeling in classrooms. Teachers expressed frustration at children going to pull-out programs for speech, ESL, special education, music lessons, chorus, band, and gifted programs throughout the school day. The regular classroom teachers stated that they could not keep up with the students' instruction because of the fragmentation of the school day. One fifth-grade teacher who complained the most about the airport philosophy became an inclusion pilot volunteer the second year. She expressed her satisfaction by sharing that the 1994-1995 school year was the first year in 5 that she felt she had control of her primary responsibility—teaching all students in her class.

Parental input was helpful in planning expansion of the inclusion pilots. Information was gathered by survey from parents of both disabled and nondisabled students in the two inclusion classes. Nineteen parents returned the survey: 6 parents out of 10 disabled students, and 13 parents of 41 nondisabled children. The results indicated that parents were satisfied with their children's education in a team-teaching environment. Parents of both disabled and nondisabled children were pleased with the extra attention given to their children and stated that having more than one teacher in the room helped their children learn. Eighteen parents reported a desire for a team-teaching classroom for their children next year, and just one parent stated that she would prefer having a child in a typical classroom with only one teacher, although no reason was given.

Parents of nondisabled children in the inclusive classrooms requested more consistent communication about the inclusion classrooms. If a parent had attended the open house and teacher conference in September and October of the year, information was shared. However, for parents who were unable to attend, the only way they knew that there was more than one teacher in the class was by student reporting. Parents stated that if information was shared before school started, they could have asked their children better questions about their teachers.

At a board of education presentation on the inclusion pilots in January 1995, 75 teachers, 6 building administrators, and 2 district administrators, as well as speech therapists, school social workers, and school psychologists shared information regarding inclusive education. A short videotape was shown, taken from activities in all elementary pilots. At the end of the presentation, no one could identify who the included children were in the tape. This pointed out the success of the pilot programs from the professional staff's—and more importantly, from the children's—point of view. All disabled children were on the tape, and no one could identify these children by how students interacted with one another or how team teachers worked with students.

Again, it is important to note that decisions made for including disabled students were on an individual basis. The number of students in one class receiving push-in services were limited to five because the IEP was not different in describing services needed. (Resource support and speech therapy have a ratio of five students to one special education teacher or speech therapist.) Services were provided in the regular classroom, not a special education classroom.

Administrative Responsibilities

A significant administration concern for principals is the commitment of personnel and the impact on the building's schedule. Teacher duties, preparation times, coordination of lunch or electives for team teachers, and the coordination of conference days and collaboration of staff members in the school are difficult time management issues. Staff inservice training programs need to be implemented for all staff, whether they are involved in team teaching or traditional class configurations.

The central administration commitment must allow building and district-level administrators to plan supportive training sessions throughout the year. The time and money involved can be coordinated but must be consistent with support promised to staff. Teachers who team taught in the pilot programs described above used their own time in addition to scheduled shared planning time. Administrative support and assistance is necessary and can be accomplished through visits to the classroom, training workshop attendance, and staff meetings. Too often, staff meetings are used to discuss necessary bureaucratic details. If the administrator can get staff to accept and respond to mundane tasks by memo, faculty meetings can be used for discussions of educational practice by teachers. Information shared here will assist teachers in their goal of helping all students learn.

Staff Development

Staff training should include visitations to programs that can demonstrate alternative methods of instruction, information-sharing workshops, and time to talk with colleagues in and across grade and subject areas. Substitutes can be used once a month for team teachers to plan program components. Two substitutes can cover two classrooms for one half-day each, giving two teams of teachers the ability to evaluate and plan lessons.

Inclusion is staff intensive because team-teaching or coteaching collaboration mandates a concentration of staff working together, requiring a redistribution of resources in a school and within a school district. However, benefits for all students in classrooms with more than one teacher are significant, and educational initiatives should focus on helping children become better learners. Teachers who are able to reach a diverse student population by sharing resources should be congratulated for their efforts. The commitment of time from the district for teacher collaboration and the commitment of time that coteachers offer are an asset to any school setting. The efforts of these teachers should be recognized and encouraged.

4

Teaching Strategies for
Students With Varied Needs

Educational Tools for Inclusion

Inclusive education focuses on a combination of best practices in education, including cooperative learning, peer tutoring, and community building in classrooms and schools. Teaching strategies for inclusive settings are synonymous with effective teaching strategies used in any area of education.

Multiage Classrooms

Multiage classrooms are becoming a part of restructuring elementary schools nationwide (Anderson & Pavan, 1992; Black, 1994). Multiage grouping drops traditional grade-level parameters to teach children based on individual needs, giving students time to develop skills. The primary focus is to individualize instruction so that children learn without the stress of achievement on traditional assessment tools, scheduled at certain times by grade expectations. This evolution results from knowledge of teachers and administrators that children learning at different rates is an acceptable concept. Students are allowed to progress at their own rate without fear of failure.

Students feel success by learning skills and working with peers in a variety of problem-solving activities. Working with children of differing abilities and ages is beneficial to all children in the class or school. Teachers are able to plan activities to assist student growth based on knowledge of students' skills, not goals of expected knowledge within a certain time frame. This allows teachers to be creative, plan collaboratively, and work toward helping individual students achieve individual goals.

Curriculum Mapping

Curriculum mapping is supporting educational reform initiatives. Teachers are working on teams in buildings and in districts to bridge curricular needs. Identification of what is being taught, in what grade level, and by whom is being looked at to plan more effectively for student outcomes (Jacobs, 1989). Interdisciplinary curriculum designs support teaching a diverse student population, which is supportive of inclusive goals.

Portfolio Assessment

Portfolio assessment is a way of building meaningful educational measures (Vavrus, 1990). Portfolios of student work are compiled, documenting a student's experience and accomplishments. Performance-based education is used, in which students think their way through a project using critical analysis, problem-solving techniques, and outcomes-based, integrated curricula. The purpose of assessment is to promote effective education with the active participation of the student. An evaluation model that assesses the ability of students to solve problems, make judgments, communicate, gather information, and work collaboratively with peers supports accountability concerns in schools. These educational philosophies are supportive of educational change initiatives and inclusion.

Students do not need to be labeled "gifted, disabled, or limited-English-proficient" for teachers and support personnel to identify strengths and weaknesses of students or to design appropriate educational goals and expectations. Teachers need the support and resources available to them to work with students to enhance educational opportunities and encourage learning through activities and experiences facilitated in school settings.

Team Teaching

Strategies that assist teachers in teaching a diverse student body involve cooperative learning, peer partnering, and team or coteaching (used synonymously). Teachers are used to working in a classroom alone, and training is required to enhance team teaching.

To team teach effectively, a clear understanding of what team teaching is and how to achieve its goal is necessary. Two teachers plan and deliver lessons together, and they share responsibility for teaching all students in a team-teaching situation. However, teachers could take turns being the instructor or split the class into groups, or one teacher could work with a few students requiring more help while the other teacher instructs the rest of the class. Most important, the teachers need to understand and share a commonality of philosophical educational practices, want to work cooperatively, and be willing to spend time planning collaboratively. It takes time to develop a positive team-teaching situation. Teachers who choose to team teach with a colleague will make the effort to create a successful classroom environment for students. Volunteers should be recruited, and time must be allotted by administrators to support the development of a shared learning environment.

Team-Teacher Training

Professionals working in the school system need training to support educational restructuring. Teachers' roles will be redefined, and inservice training to support the process is required for a successful transition.

Team teaching and shared planning time allow teachers to develop collective standards of practice (Darling-Hammond, 1992; Schattman & Benay, 1992). This supports professionalism and the ability of teachers to share knowledge. Teams are powerful tools for problem solving and providing support for team members.

There are differing needs of various school professionals (special and regular educators, principals, and pupil personnel workers) because they approach problems from different backgrounds, training, attitudes, and purposes (Bardon, 1993). Teachers need to be comfortable with having disabled students in their classrooms. Students with disabilities cannot just be physically placed into regular classrooms (Moskowitz, 1988; Zigmond & Baker, 1990). Encouraging staff members to ask questions and receive answers without passing judgment are vital communication links that help children. The teacher, with support, must be comfortable manipulating the curriculum and environment to meet the needs of students. Understanding that all children can benefit from a multisensory approach to learning will assist teachers in providing a conducive learning environment for all students.

Team teaching between a classroom teacher and a special educator allows two professionals to plan effective curriculum adaptations for children. Collaboration between professionals affects the ability of all students to gain skills from the classroom. Frequently, teachers believe that the training for special education teachers is significantly different from that for elementary teachers. However, it is important to note that this is a myth. College and university training programs for special educators through the early 1990s differed from elementary and secondary training programs by one to three courses over 4 years. Additionally, special education teachers in many states are certified K-12, with little preparation specifically at one level or another. For example, in New York, a teacher with special education certification (K-12) can be assigned to teach primary special education or high school special education. A particular teacher may have worked only with fourth-grade students in student teaching but is then assigned to a high school program. It is not unusual for teachers to say that "the special education teacher is better trained" without clearly knowing or understanding that that is not always true. In fact, many times, the regular education teacher is better trained in a particular age, grade, or subject area.

Team-Teaching Strategies

In the classroom, a compilation of activities that can be used by individuals, pairs of students, or small groups independently is helpful. If student progress is not as anticipated, teachers can work with some students while others have content-appropriate games or extra-credit activities easily at hand for reinforcement and review. These can be coordinated by monthly themes in each subject area so that, again, flexibility for the diversity of learners is planned for and student learning is maximized.

Primary Level. At the primary level (kindergarten and first grade), learning centers can be created for the classroom that will provide activities that can be directed by either teachers or students. The center may involve math manipulatives, pattern building, computers, cut-and-paste activities, imaginary play centers, listening centers, and tactile play areas involving rice or water play. In each of these centers, developmental skills can be incorporated by monthly themes, along with color and letter sounds, holidays, seasons, or other concepts on which the class has focused throughout the year.

Children can select activities by having picture clues or words, when appropriate, that indicate centers on a worksheet. There should be two to four choices on a page. If a center is to be chosen by picture, the youngest child can circle or mark the center he or she chooses. This information can be collected, and teachers can manipulate the learning environment so that all children are guided to every center throughout a specified time frame. This becomes an evaluation component for each child.

At the elementary level (second through fifth grade), similar centers can be set up in math, computer, science, language arts, and reading areas in the room. Additionally, pencil-and-paper activities and concept reinforcement can be designated in color-coded folders so that students know how to get an activity without disrupting teachers, when appropriate. For example, a two-pocket folder can be used to set up a variety of activities. If library pocket cards are glued to the inside of the folder and marked with short vowel sound words, a set of insert cards can be made so that students have to sort the word cards into the correct pocket. There can be a sheet indicating the correct sorting so that students can assist themselves or one another in proofing their work. This system works well for numerous types of curriculum-based concept development at various grade and age levels.

Setting up the centers involves a lot of planning and hard work initially, but once established, they can be used by many students over a period of years. The flexibility that these activities give teachers in managing diverse learners in the classroom, whether or not team teaching is a classroom component, is significant. The students like seeing changes in activities each month, and if four to six centers are available each month in a few subject areas, students in groups, pairs, or individually can work on reinforcing learning in a fun, independent way. Elementary-aged students can record their own progress if an evaluation for each center is provided.

One teacher who transferred to an elementary school from a high school setting spent a year developing classroom resources as described above. She acknowledged the difficulty and amount of time involved in creating this concept for her classroom. However, after 4 years, she has developed an extensive library of activities that colleagues in the building borrow and use.

In an intermediate elementary school, Grades 3 through 5, teachers in the Monticello Central School District asked if they could create a class for inservice credit in which a teacher who used many literature-based centers could assist colleagues in developing a school-based library of resources. These centers were similar to those described above and focused on the use of trade books in the school. The district committed to paying for the materials, and teachers received an inservice credit for the 10-hour class they created. The six teachers who requested this task force provided resources for 22 staff members. Additional staff members requested that another class be created the following year so that the library of support materials for students could continue to grow.

Middle and High School Level. At the middle and high school level, where classes are typically departmentalized and scheduled for a period of an average of 40 minutes, team teaching creates a slightly different capacity for flexibility than can be planned in the earlier grades. Goals are delineated by subject areas and course specifications because classes begin to require minimum competency achievement levels. However, with careful planning and collaboration, successful team teaching can positively affect students.

One or two classes can be team taught and can use the strategies discussed. An additional component revolves around the concept of integrated curriculum. The collaboration between grade-level teachers can result in the coordination of content themes that meet all subject requirements and present information to students in a coordinated way.

For example, seventh-grade teachers can integrate reading and English with social studies, science, and the math curriculum. If ancient Egypt is the theme in social studies, math instruction can be with Egyptian symbols, and reading and English activities can be geared toward Egyptian themes. Coordination across the curriculum enables teachers to coordinate lessons and assist content acquisition by reinforcement throughout the segments of the students' day.

This concept also can be achieved by pairing subjects, if all subjects cannot be included. For example, reading and social studies, and

English and science, can be connected. This way, only two teachers coordinate themes, but two are better than none. Alternatives will emerge as teachers think of ways to assist themselves in teaching diverse learners and evaluating students' responses to planned activities.

The premises of multicultural education include four descriptors that are parallel to inclusive goals. These are to provide opportunities for all children to learn, develop an awareness among teachers and students, emphasize differences in instruction and curriculum, and create opportunities for parental and community involvement.

Teachers can provide students with problem-centered lessons that encourage children to work together, solve problems, and provide hands-on learning in the classroom. A wide variety of classroom materials should be available to students. Displays of students' work in the classroom and the school should be highlighted.

Teachers need to have shared goals for their shared students. The recognition of students as diverse representatives of society is important to educators, so that planning for students' classroom activities can be geared toward the goals of living and learning within a diverse society.

Planning Curriculum Changes

Cooperative learning strategies involve presenting lessons during which students can work together and help one another learn as a team. One student's strength can assist another student's weakness, and planned grouping of students by the teachers will enable students to learn without direct teacher involvement.

Curriculum adaptations can be made that enhance learning by all students (Fiore & Cook, 1994). The diversity of learners in the general classroom includes students with disabilities, at-risk students, students from different cultures and countries, and limited-English-proficiency students. The increase of class size adds an additional burden to general classroom teachers, who lack the time to teach more than the bare curriculum to a needy student population.

All professional staff members need to be involved in the selection and adaptation of curriculum materials. Typically, special education teachers meet as a department rather than with the grade or subject teams of schools. Teaching strategies for all teachers and students will be enhanced by bridging this method of planning curriculum changes. Too often, teachers in different departments discover that a lot of wasted energy has been spent by colleagues reinventing the same wheel. The time saved by proactively asking questions and coordinating staff members would be significant.

Team teachers need to work together and develop lessons by compromising and modifying instructional approaches previously used to develop a commonality in teaching a concept. Focus must be concentrated on both teachers taking a teacher role rather than that of a teacher and an aide. It is difficult to achieve, but the benefits actualized from student and teacher perspectives are worth the effort. Continual planning and modifying should be expected, and flexibility and communication are the keys to success.

Teachers have reported that planning common monthly themes assists in collaboration. The basic parameters are determined for the entire year by September. This allows teachers to focus activities within a predetermined framework and gives them the ability to make changes without altering the concepts to be taught. Themes integrate concepts, which can connect subjects throughout the academic year and from one year to the next (Curry & Temple, 1992). This is the basis for curriculum mapping, a need for connecting curricula across grades and between subject areas. Too often, the curriculum gets taught as prescribed without anyone questioning repetition, redundancy, or worth (Jacobs, 1994).

Teacher Role Clarification

Pugach and Sapon-Shevin (1987) discussed special education reform from the perspectives of teacher preparation and the education of students. They pointed out that the failure to clarify the relationship between regular and special education for the mildly handicapped student will have a negative impact on educational reform. Changes in education must encompass all aspects of schooling, and the labeling of students with disabilities must interface within the educational community from the preparation of teachers to program implementation.

One kindergarten teacher was eager to team teach with a special education teacher because a student with Down's syndrome was entering the school. Both teachers shared a developmental approach and provided a nurturing environment for young children. After 2 months of program implementation, the kindergarten teacher expressed concerns about the included child that centered on how she was supposed to have the included child at the same level as his peers and ready for first grade by the end of the school year. During the discussion, her role was clarified, and she was told that that was not an expectation of the program. The child was expected to develop skills at his ability rate, and the discussion clarified the teacher's role and expectations and allowed her to be comfortable with what she was providing for the disabled student in a developmental classroom setting. The assumption of the administrators was that she already knew this, but once the issue was raised by a concerned teacher, it was clear that the communication of roles, expectations of the teacher, and student outcomes needed to be discussed. All participants need to be comfortable with posing questions; gaining clarification; and sharing the goals of the program, the teaching, and student components.

Implementing a shared learning environment takes a lot of work, whether the team teaching is for 2 hours per day or the whole school day. Teachers must be able to tell colleagues their preferences, be open to options for content presentation, and evaluate student responses to further plan cooperative lessons.

Many teachers are unfamiliar with what colleagues teach and how subject areas are integrated. This applies to all subject and curricular areas and is significant between regular and special educators. The mystique of what a "specialist" does in the classroom often drives the need for the "expertise" of the titled person.

Based on survey results I compiled in 1992, classroom teachers believe that special education teachers are much better trained than are regular classroom teachers (Aefsky, 1994). Teachers were surprised to find out that training was minimally different. Teachers shared that by having smaller classes and fewer curriculum-directed goals, special education teachers could help children learn more effectively. The fact that special education teachers work from an individual education plan for each student integrated with curricular goals gives special education teachers a flexibility that regular education teachers feel they do not have; it is commonly believed that teaching requires evaluation of specified curricular, not individual, goals. Changing the ways in which children are evaluated allows teachers to work with children rather than teach predetermined assessment criteria.

Changes in Teacher Certification

Certification requirements are beginning to change at the college and state levels so that all teachers are better trained in content areas and no distinction is made between regular and special education teachers. In 1993, three universities in the country had teaching programs that did not separate disciplines of special and regular education. This concept is beginning to emerge in additional colleges and universities across the country.

In September 1994, the New York Board of Regents circulated a draft memo regarding changing certification requirements for teachers of disabled students. The memo said that staff representing seven states—Connecticut, Maine, Massachusetts, New Hampshire, New York, Rhode Island, and Vermont—met and developed a common set of competencies for teachers of disabled students. Knowledge, skills, and understanding will be the premise for the certification requirements in all of the seven states as of 1997. The certification offices in each state involved with elementary, middle, secondary, and continuing education have also been involved as active partners in determining certification changes based on the same principles for all teachers.

School Climate

The entire school staff's involvement in planning team-taught, inclusive classrooms is supportive of all students. Teachers need to be able to express their desire or lack of interest in becoming a team teacher. If the staff, including the administration, allows professionals to express their choices without fear of repercussion, professionals will assess their own strengths and weaknesses, they will support each other within the school, and all students will benefit. For example, if there are six second-grade classes, two teachers may want to team teach an inclusive class. The other four teachers may be willing to have higher caseloads to enable the team-taught class to plan a new program effectively. Teachers may be able to assist the scheduling of lunches and electives to facilitate shared planning times for team teachers. If teachers can choose not to participate in inclusive pilots, they will likely support colleagues by cooperating in the planning within the school.

5

Communicating Inclusion Programs and Goals

Communication is a necessity for teachers, both throughout the school environment and with the community. Communication facilitates positive influences in establishing strong relationships in the school and community (Lev & Lev, 1992). Positive communication between parents and teachers, special and general educators, and administration is the backbone of achieving a flow of accurate information.

Communication Concerns

Inclusion programs have been unsuccessful because of a lack of training for teachers, hasty response by schools to perceived legal pressures, lack of understanding by parents and professionals of what inclusion should be, and a lack of support for staff from the administration and board of education. To support all students in the school, administrators must understand the educational objectives of inclusive education. Fred Brown, President of the National Association of Elementary School Principals, sent a letter that was published nationally in an Ann Landers column on December 14, 1994 ("Male virgin's 'catch' sees"). The gist of the letter indicated the frustration of principals in dealing with students who display acting-out behaviors, and Mr. Brown stated that IDEA "makes it virtually impossible to discipline or expel these children even if they become violent. Nor can they be expelled if they come to school with weapons." This was not an accurate statement, yet its national publication further provided incorrect information to fuel the fires that separation is better for students with disabilities. Generalized statements such as this hinder all educators, parents, and administrators in their ability to help all students learn. Educators and parents of all children are needed to support children in schools. Resources in schools need to support students' diverse needs. Children and staff safety are a priority, but educators must understand the need for educating every child. IDEA supports these concepts, and understanding the intent of this law is vital to all educators.

Building Shared Goals

A purposeful association of parents, teachers, administrators, and students creates a partnership of school personnel and parents that facilitates children's success. Identifying a unified goal clarifies a mission toward which home and school work together. Developing a strong sense of community is important for all children, staff, and parents (Everett, 1992; Redding, 1991). Establishing caring, supportive, and educationally productive classrooms encourages positive, inclusive education for all students. Parental involvement fosters an informed support group that has input into the shared educational strategies used with its children. Schools should be tailored to meet the developmental needs of children and should support a child-centered approach to teaching and learning.

Leaders' Roles

Building a sense of community in each classroom, each school, and the community requires a conscious effort by school staff, administrators, and parents. Wherry (1992) states that parental involvement is important. He suggests that someone must take the role of ensuring parental invitations to school events and meetings. Encouraging the students to work at involving their parents in schools can be a useful tool.

Inclusion can be defined in many different ways. A massive public relations and marketing plan needs to be implemented, and correct information needs to be disseminated. Teachers, parents, and administrators need to have access to a forum in which questions and concerns can be addressed. Staff inservice training, pilot programs, and staff and parent input should be focused on as facilitators of this process.

An appropriate leadership responsibility is to focus on diversity in the schools. Regardless of difference, be it a disabling condition, race, gender, or culture, schools must become places where all children learn harmoniously with others. Teachers must learn to work cooperatively with differences among philosophies, other staff members, parents, and administrators. The school climate must be conducive to supporting all learners in the school community, focusing on children but acknowledging parents, teachers, administration, and community members.

Goals 2000 is a national comprehensive strategy for improving public education (Bush, 1991). Strong leadership, a focus on building-level planning and support, and the shared responsibility of all to teach all students are priorities in achieving system goals.

At the district level, communication between the board of education and the central administration must be clear in relation to goals of inclusive education. Parameters must be set by defining goals, and this information must be disseminated to parents, administrators, school staff, and community members. When information is presented, the leadership of the district should provide goals consistent with state plans for America 2000 (Bush, 1991). A suggestion for enhancing the board of education members' understanding of inclusion is to set up visitations to classes with and without included students. Let the visitors try to ascertain who the included students are in each class. If this is not possible, present a program with videotapes of classes for the same purpose. Communication of restructuring goals to teachers, parents, and community members can be established by similar methods.

Separation of inclusion as a special education program is not conducive to sound educational practice. We as educators need to learn from our mistakes. Every time a mandate for the education of disabled students has been introduced, it has become the responsibility of the special education administrators to inform building administrators. This enables a separation of children by distinct labels.

Nothing is more offensive than hearing educators talk about "special ed kids." No one can define all children who are disabled in one category, yet again and again, educators in buildings, districts, and in national media forums use this terminology. Be reminded that many children in this country identified as "special ed kids" have average or better intelligence and are receiving support in the school building; people who use this term could not identify half of the students thus labeled. We must learn to communicate with each other in a more productive manner before we can communicate better with others.

At the building level, a leader must clearly understand the mission and be willing to drive activities to communicate what is happening. Plans for growth and evaluation mechanisms to be used by staff to reach program goals must be facilitated. This is consistent with goals of site-based management. Decentralizing school management is based on the premise that educational decisions are best made at the building level. The concept of site-based management supports individual schools' being responsible and accountable for school decisions in budget, personnel, and program decisions (McLaughlin & Warren, 1992). Facilitating a team approach in a school results in better commitment to tasks, the team, and the organization. A higher level of trust is obtained between staff and administrators, among staff, between parents and school staff, and between teachers and students. Mutual respect for differences evolves, providing an environment conducive to all members of the school community.

The educational leaders in a district need to structure organizational change. To accomplish this, leaders should spend as much time posing questions as they spend attempting to answer them (Davis, 1982). This will facilitate baby steps toward guided change, with a focus on experimentation. I once heard a principal presenting at a staff development meeting, and her point hit home. She stated that her teachers are encouraged to try anything once, as long as it's legal and safe. This gives teachers permission to be creative thinkers in a nonthreatening way. Students benefit from successes and mistakes because follow-up discussion assists teachers and the administrator in developing changes for increased student learning. If administrators pose the right questions, stimulating thought and experimentation, the morale of the school is heightened and everyone benefits.

Administrators at the building and district levels need to continue to be advocates for maintaining a full continuum of special education services, which does not indicate a lack of support for inclusive practices (Blackman, 1993). It is just as important for eligibility committees to recommend that students be placed in a more restrictive setting, based on individual students' needs and the least restrictive environment (LRE) rules, as it is to place disabled students in a regular classroom with supplemental support services, based on LRE. To dump all disabled students into a program or to keep all disabled students from a program clearly indicates the lack of understanding and knowledge about special education services for disabled students.

Administrators also need to let parents of all students in the school know that they are concerned about the education of the children. The parents of disabled and nondisabled children need to feel that both teachers and educational structural change address the needs of all students (Idstein, 1994). Discussions of inclusion should focus on meeting the needs of a diverse student population, and parents must be informed and have input into suggested school improvement plans.

Structural change should take place on a districtwide level, and common philosophical parameters must be established. School-based specifics can be different from one another within the districtwide philosophy. It is important to share that differences are expected so that parents of students in one family attending different schools will support a variety of measures that are necessary to meet the educational needs of all students. Teachers at different grade levels also need to expect differences to exist among individual students as well as in subject areas and grade levels. Having prior knowledge that differences will occur and that flexibility in program delivery is expected will minimize fear of failure and maximize teacher and parent creativity and experimentation in reaching specified goals.

Building Support for Change

A strategic plan must be determined, actualized, changed, re-actualized, and cyclically facilitated. The ability to accept change is very difficult. Change is an ongoing process. The process must involve all participants, encourage a degree of trial and error, and support innovative ideas. Learning organizations allow people to continually expand their capacities in working toward results they truly desire, where new ideas are nurtured, and where people are continually learning how to learn together (Senge, 1990). If leaders can get 20% of the staff to jump on the bandwagon of change, that 20% becomes the catalyst for an additional 40% of support. Building trust and collaboration between and among individuals, and enabling change to occur, are roles that educational leaders must take.

Surveys are a positive way of collecting information to begin a change process. The building leader should present a vision or goal statement at a general faculty meeting, follow up at smaller department meetings, and ask for volunteer building representatives. This core group can develop an anonymous survey, gathering input from staff. The results of the survey can identify components of a needs assessment with which the whole school community, including parents, can be involved. The questions on the needs assessment should involve staff concerns and both positive and negative aspects of good educational practices, and a school mission statement can be derived from the responses. If the questions are posed well, the results will support a need for improvement that can be integrated with goals of inclusion as a key in bridging inclusive practices with current educational initiatives.

Teacher Support

Teachers need to have access to information regarding inclusive classrooms and the resulting benefits and/or detriments to both disabled and nondisabled children. In one published study, a pilot program in Minnesota was looked at for this purpose (Sharpe, York, & Knight, 1994). Including five moderately disabled students in a regular classroom and following from Grades 1 through 4, the academic performance of nondisabled students in the classes was assessed. The results indicated that there were no negative academic or behavioral effects on nondisabled classmates in the inclusive classroom.

It is important to note that in this study, one to five disabled students were included in one of three classes based on individual decisions of the LRE requirement. All children included in this study previously had been placed in self-contained special education classes. The achievement of nondisabled peers was compared to other class results on standardized assessment tools in reading, math, and spelling. Effort and conduct was compared by teacher report card results.

The authors pointed out that more comparable studies need to be compiled before generalizing results. However, the dissemination of information-in-progress to teachers and parents can assist educational leaders in building team support.

Teachers also need to have access to all available information regarding disabled children in their classrooms. Although the privacy of individuals whose records are obtained from a multidisciplinary team assessment must be maintained, that does not mean that teachers cannot read the information compiled. There is no basis for having educated file cabinets, where records are placed and never read. The information about learning styles, strengths and weaknesses, and skill levels of individual students gained from an evaluation is of significant classroom use. All teachers and support staff working with disabled students should have knowledge of and access to information, as well as copies of the student's individual educational plan (IEP).

Student Support

Children value social behaviors differently than do adults (Cullinan, Sabornie, & Crossland, 1992). Children admire peers who are helpful, good at games, talkative, nonaggressive, and successful in academics. Teachers can assist students' interaction with each other, including disabled peers, by focusing on the strengths in a social area for student success. Placing a disabled student with a nondisabled peer might encourage interaction. Directing an activity in which, for instance, a disabled student helps a nondisabled peer work on a computer can build friendships. Disabled and nondisabled children need a sense of belonging and to feel valued as members of their school and community (Buswell & Schaffner, 1992).

Parent Support

Parents can be key to communicating change in a positive way. As students' needs change, parental awareness and active participation of parents in the change process must be acknowledged. Increased parental involvement is a goal stated in the America 2000 plan (Bush, 1991). A school that requests parental involvement through volunteering, shared activities sponsored through community groups and parent organizations, and other mechanisms of ongoing communication sees great benefit for staff and students.

Building communication bridges between home and school supports students maximally. Teachers should not wait until a problem in student behavior or academic achievement exists to coordinate efforts between school and home. It is important to establish a mutual respect for each other's role from the beginning of a student's school career in kindergarten and to continue this partnership throughout graduation from high school. If school administrators and staff value parental input and recognize the importance of collaboration between the adults in a child's life, the child will be supported to perform to his or her ability.

Teachers need to recognize that the range of parental support for students will vary, and they should attempt to help the school community provide ways to support the individual teacher-parent relationship. It is common for teachers to talk about the lack of response from parents, yet conversations about a child often focus on the lack of homework completed and the frustrations of not accomplishing school goals. Educators in all rural, suburban, and urban communities recognize the impact of societal issues and problems with traditional family support for youth. As educators, we need to change our expectations of the parent relationship with school because of these factors.

We have students in school for 6½ to 7 hours per day. We know that many children go home to houses without adult supervision, yet we continue to expect home support for school assignments that require a lot of adult supervision for students. This occurs in all grade levels because projects, papers, worksheets, and reading assignments often necessitate adult support for material collection and completion. How can we continue to ask students to complete tasks at home while stating that we recognize changes affecting students in their homes? We need to collaboratively allow students to achieve success in spite of their individual home situations by maximizing their school day. If a teacher knows a young child will not get help with homework, instead of assigning the homework, the teacher should allow the child time during the school day to work on tasks that show his or her knowledge. As school progresses, children should be taught that part of their responsibility is to complete assignments at home, and they should receive support for this in school. For example, if teachers require specific report covers, the school or teacher should make them available to students. It is unfair to tell students that no matter what, the information gathered must be presented in a format requiring one particular cover, or else the student will fail the assignment regardless of work presented. As ludicrous as it may sound, this happens in high school classes in 1994. Denying a student credit after completing an assignment because the cover was the wrong type is improper. Maybe there were no funds to buy the cover, maybe there was no transportation to get the cover, or maybe there were no covers available in the local store.

Students should be accountable for work they are assigned, but their efforts at completing the work must also be recognized. A kindergarten child who has no crayons at home may be admonished for not completing the assigned homework, even if the teacher sent home supplies at the beginning of the school year. Sometimes a child loses items, or else a sibling takes them, and if adult supervision and support is not strong in a household, how can we hold the child responsible for things out of his or her control? School staffs need to recognize these issues and, rather than expect less of the children, devise ways that children can demonstrate their knowledge and effort during school-controlled hours. Parents will begin to see and understand that school personnel want to help their children, not punish parents based on a preconceived value system. A parent of one of my students during my first year of teaching once told me that my suggestions were fine for the classroom; once I was a parent, however, I would realize that what teachers thought should be done to support a child during nonschool hours and the answers to the question of why parents did not control the home environment in the same manner as in school would become apparent. Sixteen years have passed, and I often think how correct this parent was in her statement of fact. Once the realization is accepted, school hours become the source of directed expectations for students. If a student has support at home, it is wonderful, but if not, students can still achieve and gain support from school personnel.

Although educators recognize and adjust expectations for homework, we need to work simultaneously with parents of all students to the best of our shared ability. Educators talk about how parents of young children are more responsive than are parents of high school students. Some teachers have reached success in communicating and working with parents of all students, regardless of age. However, educators' expectations of parents of older students may be different. If the expectations of teachers increase, parental response may increase, generating results that will assist all students.

One successful way of maximizing the parent-school connection is the implementation of a parent university program. This program can develop strong bonds among school, parents, and the community. A parent university program provides courses through workshops on a quarterly basis for parents of students in the school district. The goals are to provide communication among parents, school, and community; share information that will enable students to have a positive school experience; and foster cooperative growth among parents and teachers to help our children succeed at home, in school, and in our community.

Workshops are presented by community people, school staff, and consultants. For example, if the school district has a DARE (drug awareness) program, a workshop may be presented by the DARE coordinator so that parents have a clear understanding of that program's goal. Another workshop may be presented by the financial aid adviser of a college, who will assist parents in applying for grants and student loans. One workshop may present information regarding developmental skills, disabilities, minimum competency course expectations, study skills as a way of helping students with homework, and social skills development. The list is endless.

The key difference between a parent university program and typical parent workshops is its focus on learning, not the remediation of a problem. Many times, school districts offer workshops to parents whose children are exhibiting problems in school, and classes are scheduled for parents of children with discipline or attendance problems. The parent university program is planned so that a multitude of options are available to parents on the class night. One- to 2-hour sessions are scheduled, and two classes can be attended by parental choice. The announcement of the night's offerings should contain registration forms and allow the parents to sign up for chosen classes independently of school staff's suggestions. The parent university booklet is prepared like a college registration brochure.

This kind of program has been offered in school districts in New York, Arizona, and Texas. In Texas, the district program reviewed was in a very poor, rural district. In Arizona, the district program reviewed was in a very wealthy, suburban district. In New York, the program reviewed was in a middle-income district located on the outskirts of suburbia. Parental attendance in all three districts was very good, and parental evaluation was supportive of increasing program offerings. In the wealthy district, nominal fees were charged.

In the poorer districts, no fees were charged, and babysitting and transportation was provided to some participants. Interagency collaboration was maximized, and the community participated in building school partnerships.

Parents of disabled and nondisabled children have shared concerns about inclusive practices. All parent expect teachers to have goals for their children. No one wants to limit any child's ability by setting expectations too low (Rist, 1970). Parents want their children to learn, communicate, feel for themselves and others, and interact well with other people (Oberti, 1993). All children deserve the chance to be the best they can be regardless of disabling conditions.

Achieving parent-teacher collaboration is the responsibility of both the school and parents of students. Administrators need to have a focused parent involvement plan, involving the coordination of school volunteers, parent-teacher conferences (when parents can attend), workshops for parents and teachers, building-level support teams, and telephone availability for teachers.

Parents of disabled children who are included may need additional school staff support to be comfortable. In the Monticello school pilots, teachers talked about team teaching and disabled students being included at parent orientation, open house events, and at individual parent-teacher conferences of students in the inclusive classes. Parents dropped in to see the class, and although some parents expressed concern, by the third month of pilot implementation, parents of both disabled and nondisabled children appeared comfortable and saw benefits to having two teachers in the classroom.

Parents of nondisabled students in the primary school where the kindergarten inclusive pilot was implemented but whose children were not in the inclusive class were heard talking negatively about inclusion throughout the community. Parents discussed how educational gains would be minimized for "regular" students and talked with teachers who were also concerned. These teachers were not involved in task force activities. The lack of information shared with the school community affected the successful communication of what inclusive education meant for identified students. It is important that all school personnel be informed, allowed to ask questions, and allowed to share concerns, even if only a limited number of staff are directly involved in inclusive education. Communicating effectively to all stakeholders allows for support to and for all staff and students.

Teachers need to be flexible in allowing visitations to the classroom and encouraging parents to be comfortable in the school setting. Once parents are comfortable in the school, they will be more comfortable building relationships with individual teachers, asking questions, and planning solutions together. If parents do not feel that their input is heard by teachers, there will be limited support for the child between parents and school.

Celebrating Education

Tolerance of others is not a new concept, nor is inclusion. Inclusion is sound educational practice. Classrooms need to nurture students, and all children need to learn how to be cooperative learning partners with peers in academic and social areas of development. All teachers have varying teaching skills, and all children have learning strengths and weaknesses. Children want and need to be part of their minisociety in neighborhood schools. Schools are for all children, including those with disabilities, those speaking different languages, and those from culturally different and environmentally deprived homes.

Schools need to focus on their primary purpose—teaching children to be members of a democratic society. Support for teachers, administrators, and parents are important components, but the clients of schools are children! Let us help children to be members of one society, not one where labels and fear of the unknown in one another drives separation of the whole. Schools are the place to teach acceptance of differences, and having young children learning about one another is the place to start fostering a caring world.

The Language of Inclusion

Inclusion as a concept will have greater success of becoming an accepted part of sound educational practice if a commonality of language is used by professionals. There *must* be communication linkages between educators to begin the process of understanding. Educators need to start thinking of themselves as educators of *all* children. Particular jobs should describe parameters and distinctions between educators, not label the students taught.

Inclusion should not be considered a special education initiative. The terms *special education* and *regular education* should no longer be used. All children are special and have special needs. I have defined the "Pollyanna Principle" as a philosophy where everyone accepts all people as individuals without assigning values based on classification by any descriptor. This philosophy can enable educators to speak a common language, support colleagues' decisions, and be able and willing to teach all children.

Unfortunately, since 1975, federal mandates have dictated services to students based on a system of labeling children and teachers. This system invoked the necessary specialization of students and teachers into categories of gifted, special needs, ESL, or Chapter I. Teachers in classrooms were told that if a child fit into a category, the child was to be instructed by the corresponding specialist. Classroom teachers were directed to separate learners into groups in and out of the classroom for instruction.

Inclusion is turning the tables after 15 unsuccessful years of teaching children in a fragmented school society. We are asking professionals (teachers, administrators, and support staff) to change their roles.

As educators look to provide services to children without labels, educators need to stop delineating ideology by new labels. What purpose is served when proponents of multiage classrooms, integrated curriculum, whole language learning, portfolio assessment, cultural diversity, multiculturalism, inclusion, special education, and diverse learning styles all describe similar ways of educating children? All support sound educational practices for schools. If the educational community can coordinate research and practitioner efforts, children will benefit.

We must change the language to support the role change! Educators need to focus on the current and future needs of the children. Educational leaders need to assist schools, teachers, and parents in seeing that change in how we teach our children is necessary. No one can expect overnight change; however, it is imperative that all educators begin asking questions and altering strategies and methods so that diverse student needs can be met by the experts that all school districts have—the teachers! Support must be provided so that teachers can experiment and create new ways of educating our youth. The best practice in education may be to plan for schools to assign no more than 20 students to each class.

Teachers want to help children succeed. The tools are available in spite of difficult sociological times. The separation of schools from societal issues will not occur, nor should it. Teaching students to survive with others is crucial to planning the educational goals for all students.

No single recipe for inclusion makes sense for all children in all school districts. But remember, inclusion does not decrease the educational options for students with disabilities; rather, it increases the options for all students!

References

Aefsky, F. (1994). *A team teaching model for the inclusion of special-needs kindergarten children with nonhandicapped peers.* Unpublished doctoral dissertation, Nova Southeastern University, Fort Lauderdale, FL.

Americans with Disabilities Act of 1990, Pub. L. No. 101-336, § 2, 104 Stat. 328 (1991).

Anderson, R., & Pavan, B. (1992). *Nongradedness: Helping it to happen.* Lancaster, PA: Technomic.

Ayers, G. (1994). Statistical profile of special education in the United States. *Teaching Exceptional Children, 26*(3), 1-4.

Bardon, J. (1993). Viewpoints on multidisciplinary teams in schools. *School Psychology Review, 12*(2), 186-189.

Black, S. (1994). *Staying focused on the children.* Peterborough, NH: Society for Developmental Education.

Blackman, H. (1993). An administrator's perspective on inclusion. *Exceptional Parent, 23*(7), 22-24.

Board of Education of East Windsor v. Diamond, 808 F. 2d 987, 36 Ed. Law Rep. 1136 (3d Cir.) (1986).

Board of Education of Hendrick Hudson Central School District v. Rowley, 458 U.S. 176, 102 S. Ct. 3034, 73 L. Ed.2d 690, 5 Ed. Law Rep. 34 (1982).

Brown v. Board of Education, 347 U.S. 483 (1954).

Bush, G. (1991). *America 2000: An education strategy.* Washington, DC: U.S. Department of Education.

Buswell, B., & Schaffner, B. (1992). *Office of Special Education and Rehabilitative Services News in Print, 4*(4), 4-8.

Cordisco, L., & Laus, M. (1993). Individualized training in behavioral strategies for parents of preschool children with disabilities. *Teaching Exceptional Children, 25*(2), 43-46.

Council for Exceptional Children. (1993). CEC advocates "Full inclusion." *Legacy, 3* (2).

Council for Exceptional Children. (1995). *Today, 1*(9).

Courtnage, L., & Smith-Davis, J. (1987). Interdisciplinary team training: A national survey of special education teacher training programs. *Exceptional Children, 53*(5), 451-458.

Crawford, C., & Porter, G. (1992). How it happens: A look at inclusive educational practices in Canada for children and youth with disabilities. In *Health and welfare.* Toronto: G. Allan Roehr Institutes.

Cronin, M., Slade, D., Bechtel, C., & Anderson, P. (1992). Home-school partnerships: A cooperative approach to intervention. *Intervention in School and Clinic, 27*(5), 286-292.

Cullinan, D., Sabornie, E., & Crossland, C. (1992). Social mainstreaming of mildly handicapped students. *Elementary School Journal, 92*(3), 339-351.

Curry, B., & Temple, T. (1992). *Using curriculum frameworks for systemic reform.* Alexandria, VA: Association for Supervision and Curriculum Development.

Daniel R. R. v. State Board of Education, 874 F.2d 1036, 53 Ed. Law Rep. 824 (5th Cir.) (1989).

Darling-Hammond, L. (1992, November). Reframing the school reform agenda. *School Administrator, 23*(2), 22-27.

Davern, L. (1992). *The elements of inclusion.* Position paper of the Inclusive Education Project. New York: Syracuse University.

Davis, S. (1982, Winter). Transforming organizations: The key to strategy is context. *Organizational Dynamics,* pp. 105-124.

Dawson, P. (1987). Assistant secretary of education calls for more special education/regular education cooperation. *Communiqué, 15*(6), 1-3.

Early Childhood Report. (1994, February). *5*(10).

Education for All Handicapped Children Act of 1975, 89 U.S.C. 1411 (1975).

Education of the Handicapped Act. 20 U.S.C. 1471 (1986).

Everett, M. (1992, March). Developmental interdisciplinary schools for the 21st century. *Education Digest,* pp. 57-59.

Fiore, T., & Cook, R. (1994). Adopting textbooks and other materials. *Remedial and Special Education, 15*(6), 333-347.

Florida's strategic plan. (1993, December). Presented to the Exceptional Student Education Advisory Committee, Palm Beach Country, FL.

Friend, M., & Cook, L. (1992). The new mainstreaming. *Instructor, 101*(7), 30-36.

Fuchs, D., & Fuchs, L. (1994). Inclusive schools movement and the radicalization of special education reform. *Exceptional Children, 60*(4), 294-305.

Greer v. Rome City School District, 950 F. 2d 688, 71 Ed. Law Rep. 647 (11th Cir.) (1992).

Hogges, R., & Spiva, U. (1993). Educational collaboration: Achieving the readiness goal. *Florida ASCD Journal, 11,* 51-54.

Honig v. Doe, 479 U.S. 1084, 107 S. Ct. 1284, L. Ed. 2d 142 (1988).

Hopkins, D. (1990). Integrating staff development and school improvement: A study of teacher personality and school climate. In B. Joyce (Ed.), *Changing school culture through staff development* (pp. 41-67). Alexandria, VA: Association for Supervision and Curriculum Development.

Idstein, P. (1994). Swimming against the mainstream. *Education Digest, 59*(6), 23-25.

Individuals with Disabilities Education Act (IDEA), U.S.C. Title 20, § 1400 et seq. (1990).

Jacobs, H. H. (Ed.). (1989). *Interdisciplinary curriculum: Design implementation.* Alexandria, VA: Association for Supervision and Curriculum Development.

Jacobs, H. H. (1994, October). *Practical uses for curriculum mapping.* Paper presented at a workshop sponsored by the Board of Cooperative Educational Services, Sullivan County, New York.

Jenkins, J., Jewell, M., Leicester, N., Jenkins, L., & Troutner, N. (1991). Development of a school building model for educating students with handicaps and at-risk students in general education classrooms. *Journal of Learning Disabilities, 24*(5), 311-320.

Johnston v. Ann Arbor Public Schools, 569 F. Supp. 1502, 13 Ed. Law Rep. 680 (E.D. Mich.) (1983).

Landers, A. (1994, December 14). Male virgin's "catch" sees scarlet letter. *Times Herald Record*, p. 32.

Lev, J., & Lev, S. (1992). Multidisciplinary teams: The essence of empowerment. *The Forum, 18*(3), 5-7.

Lortie, D. (1975). *Schoolteacher: A sociological study.* Chicago: University of Chicago Press.

McLaughlin, M., & Warren, S. (1992). *Issues and options restructuring schools and special education programs.* College Park, MD: Westat.

Metropolitan School District of Wayne Township v. Davilla, 18 ID ELR 1226 (7th Cir.) (1991).

Miles, M. B. (1965). Planned change and organizational health: Figure and ground. In Oregon state position paper, *Change Process in the Public Schools.*

Mills v. Board of Education, 348 F. Supp. 866 (D.C.C.) (1972).

Mitchell, A. (1989). Old baggage, new visions: Shaping policy for early childhood programs. *Phi Delta Kappan, 70*(9), 664-672.

Moskowitz, F. (1988). Strategies for mainstreamed students. *Academic Therapy, 23*(5), 541-547.

Nowacek, E. (1992). Professionals talk about teaching together. *Intervention in School and Clinic, 27*(5), 262-276.

Oakland, T., Shermis, M., & Coleman, M. (1990). Teacher perceptions of differences among elementary students with and without learning disabilities in referred samples. *Journal of Learning Disabilities, 23*(8), 499-504.

Oberti, C. (1993). A parent's perspective on inclusion. *Exceptional Parent, 23*(7), 18-21.

Oberti v. Board of Education of Clementon School District, 995 F. Supp. 1204 (E.D. N.J.) (1993).

Office of Special Education. (1993, January 28). *The operational plan to accompany the Strategic Plan for Least Restrictive Environment Tenure Plan.* Report submitted to the board of education of Howard County, MD. Annapolis, MD: Author.

Pae, P. (1994, December 16). Loudon can take autistic boy out of regular class. *The Washington Post*, pp. 1, 6.

Pearpoint, J., & Forest, M. (1992). *The inclusion papers: Strategies to make it happen.* Toronto: Inclusion.

Pennsylvania Association for Retarded Citizens v. Commonwealth of Pennsylvania, 343 F. Supp. 279 (E.D. Pa.) (1972).

Pugach, M., & Sapon-Shevin, M. (1987). New agendas for special education policy. *Exceptional Children, 53*(4), 295-299.

Raywid, M. (1993). Finding time for collaboration. *Educational Leadership, 51*(1), 30-34.

Redding, S. (1991, November). Creating a school community through parental involvement. *Education Digest*, pp. 6-9.

Rehabilitation Act, #504, U.S.C., Title 29, #794 (1973).

Rist, R. (1970). Student social class and teacher expectations: The self-fulling prophecy in ghetto education. *Harvard Educational Review, 40*(3), 411-451.

Roncker v. Walter, 700 F. 2d 1058, 9 Ed. Law Rep. 827 (6th Cir.) (1983).

Sacramento City Unified School District v. Holland, 786 F. Supp. 874 (E.D. Cal.) (1992).

Salisbury, C. (1991). Mainstreaming during the early childhood years. *Exceptional Children, 58*(20), 146-154.

Schattman, R., & Benay, J. (1992). Inclusiveness transforms special education for the 1990's. *The School Administrator, 49*, 8-12.

Senge, P. (1990). *The fifth discipline.* New York: Doubleday.

Sharpe, M., York, J., & Knight, J. (1994). Effects of inclusion on the academic performance of classmates without disabilities. *Remedial and Special Education, 15*(5), 281-287.

Slavin, R., Karweit, N., & Wasik, B. (1993). Preventing early school failure: What works? *Educational Leadership, 50*(4), 10-18.

Special Education Report. (1993, March 10). *19*(5).

Sundram, C. (1990). *Special education in NYS: Parents' perspective.* Albany: New York State Commission on Quality Care for the Mentally Disabled.

U.S. Department of Education. (1993a). 15th annual report to Congress on the implementation of the Individuals With Disabilities Act. Washington, DC.

U.S. Department of Education. (1993b). *The national education goals report 1: Building a nation of leaders.* Washington, DC: Author.

U.S. Department of Education. (1991). *Delivering special education: Statistics and trends* (Contract No. RI88062007). Washington, DC: Office of Educational Research and Improvement.

U.S. Department of Education. (1994). *World Almanac and Book of Facts.* New York: Funk & Wagnalls.

Vavrus, L. (1990). Put portfolios to the test. *Instructor, 100*(1), 48-53.

Viadero, D. (1992, November 18). NASBE endorses full inclusion of disabled students. *Education Week*, pp. 1-2.

Viadero, D. (1993, April 14). Special educators' group weighs in on "full inclusion." *Education Week*, p. 5.

Wherry, J. (1992). Getting parents involved. *Vocational Education Journal, 66*(6), 49-51.

Will, M. (1987). Educating students with learning problems. *Communiqué, 15*(6), pp. 1-2.

Wilson v. Marana Unified School District, 735 F. 2nd 1178, (1984).

Wyatt v. Stickney, 334 F. Supp. 1341 (1971).

Zigmond, N., & Baker, B. (1990). Mainstream experiences for learning disabled students: Preliminary report. *Exceptional Children, 57*(2), 176-185.

CORWIN
PRESS

The Corwin Press logo—a raven striding across an open book—
represents the happy union of courage and learning. We are a
professional-level publisher of books and journals for K–12 educators, and we are committed to creating and providing resources that
embody these qualities. Corwin's motto is "Success for All Learners."